Face of Courage

DARRYl leith

By the same author:

George Pemba: Against All Odds
(Jonathan Ball & Harper Collins, 1996)

Face of Courage

A BIOGRAPHY OF
MORGAN TSVANGIRAI

Sarah Hudleston

DOUBLE
STOREY
a juta company

First published in 2005 by Double Storey Books,
a division of Juta & Co. Ltd, Mercury Crescent,
Wetton, Cape Town

ISBN 1 77013 005 5

Page layout by Claudine Willatt-Bate
Cover design by Abdul Amien
Printing by Paarl Print, Paarl

*This book is dedicated to the brave men and women
of Zimbabwe who have sacrificed their lives
and their livelihoods to fight for democracy and
take a heroic stand against tyranny*

Contents

Preface

In 1948 my parents, like so many other migrants, answered the British government's call to 'serve the Empire' and settled in Southern Rhodesia with very little more than their clothes and a few possessions.

Their early days in Bulawayo were not easy. They rented a room in the suburb of Hillside. This boasted a communal long-drop lavatory and no kitchen. All cooking was done over a small Primus stove while the fridge was crafted from an old whiskey crate, dug into the ground and covered with hay bales. This was a far cry from their sophisticated flat in London's South Kensington. However, things slowly improved and on the day my eldest brother was born, in December 1950, my father's meagre salary was doubled and life began to be more comfortable.

By December 1955, when I was born, my parents had borrowed money from my maternal grandmother, raised a mortgage, and built a house. My father, working around the country, was seldom in Bulawayo during the week so my mother, with the aid of two labourers, built our home.

Rhodesia did not have quite the apartheid regime of its neighbour to the south, but was not far from it. In truth, we lived in a schizoid society, with huge racial disparities in education facilities and employment opportunities.

In 1978, while working for a Harare Public Relations Consultancy, metal identity cards were introduced. I went to get mine. The queue was so long that I simply gave up. Without that card it has been impossible to maintain my Zimbabwean citizenship.

In 1979, just prior to the country's transition to independence, my father retired to pursue his dream of living on a boat in the Mediterranean. My parents packed up our home in Bulawayo and the family went to England, although I soon decided to return to Africa and settled in Johannesburg. In 1990 I tried to get my Zimbabwean citizenship back, but I had left it too long and was unsuccessful in my application.

Despite not being a Zimbabwean citizen, I have always kept a close eye on events in the country; not only because I have relatives still living there, but also because it is the only place where I can truly say that I feel 'at home'.

I followed the run-up to the elections in June 2000 with interest and excitement, hoping that the MDC, seemingly sprung from nowhere, would triumph. In truth, the party had grown from a united Zimbabwean trade union movement set on ending the tyranny of a corrupt leader and a government that had overstayed its welcome. Just before the country went to the polls, Morgan Tsvangirai gave his now-famous freedom speech at Rufaro Stadium in Harare. It was from this speech that my interest in the man was piqued.

In spite of my family's liberal stance, I would have to say that Morgan Tsvangirai and myself, born three years apart and of the same generation, grew up in what could be described as different countries within the same nation. Discovering who he is and what he stands for has been enlightening. Through researching his life and the modern history of the country in which he and I grew up – and which he has dedicated his life to – I have rediscovered the country of my birth.

Morgan Tsvangirai is a man who has been presented with a

seemingly insurmountable task. He is, like so many around him who have dedicated themselves to restoring Zimbabwe to a workable democracy, sacrificing his safety and that of his family. Like them, he is a person of vision and honour. Above all, he is a man of great intelligence, energy and courage, committed to letting go of the past and to forging a new future for Zimbabwe.

Sarah Hudleston
Johannesburg, April 2005

Acknowledgements

First and foremost I want to thank Morgan Tsvangirai for the time he has spent with me and the insight he has given me into the beloved country of my birth. I pray that he and his able and dedicated colleagues in the Movement for Democratic Change will be given the opportunity to put things right in Zimbabwe.

I would also like to thank my family and friends here and in England for their unequivocal support in this rather long exercise. In particular, my brother James financially supported me in the early days of researching the book, making it possible for me to stop working and to travel to Zimbabwe and back during my research.

My gratitude goes to those who kindly had me to stay on my numerous trips to Zimbabwe and to those who have filled me in on the history and background to events in Zimbabwe since 1980. In particular, I would like to thank Mike and Judy Carter who motivated me to start this project and who had me to stay on their lovely farm before it was seized from them. I would also like to thank Topper Whitehead for helping me with most of the photographs. William Bango, Morgan Tsvangirai's personal spokesperson, was extremely kind and helpful to me as was his secretary Edith Munyaka. Above all, in Zimbabwe I would like to pay tribute to Zodwa Sibanda, beloved wife of MDC vice-president Gibson Sibanda, who died at the end of 2003 after a long battle with cancer. Zodwa, who first dedicated herself to the war of liberation, turned her efforts to helping restore democracy to Zimbabwe. She helped me immeasurably.

In addition, I am grateful to Andrea Nattrass for her editorial input and to Jethro Goko for reading through an almost final draft, making suggestions in an attempt to stop me falling into a bottomless pit of litigation and correcting the Shona spelling – especially in the poem in the book's opening pages. He has been a source of encouragement to me since the end of 2002 and I thank him for it.

Finally, this book would not have happened without the support of my good friend Libby Nelson. She spent many weeks in Sydney, Australia, snatching moments from her valuable time as a mother to pore over the manuscript, making valid comments and doing a first edit that did not change my style of writing – a mean feat by anyone's standards.

Abbreviations

ANC	African National Congress
CFU	Commercial Farmers' Union
CIA	Central Intelligence Agency
CIO	Central Intelligence Organisation
Esap	Economic Structural Adjustment Programme
Jag	Justice for Agriculture
MDC	Movement for Democratic Change
MP	Member of Parliament
NCA	National Constitutional Assembly
NDP	National Democratic Party
Nepad	New Partnership for Africa's Development
NGO	Non-Governmental Organisation
OAU	Organisation of African Unity
ODA	Overseas Development Administration
RF	Rhodesian Front
UDI	Unilateral Declaration of Independence
UK	United Kingdom
UN	United Nations
US	United States
Zanla	Zimbabwe African National Liberation Army
Zanu	Zimbabwe African National Union
Zanu-PF	Zimbabwe African National Union-Patriotic Front
Zapu	Zimbabwe African People's Union
ZCTU	Zimbabwe Congress of Trade Unions
Zimcet	Zimbabwe Civic Education Trust
Zipra	Zimbabwe People's Revolutionary Army
ZUM	Zimbabwe Unity Movement

Kunge kurwa Kwotsvirizidza
Nemhandu dzenge dzasimba kwazzo,
Zvinorukudzo umire nazvo
Kubudirira hakusi Ny'ore
Ndiko kwavanhu vano unhinhi
Shingira nguva yose narini
Urambe kuti, Urambe kuti
Urambe kuti 'Handikwanisi!'

———

When the battle is fiercest
and it seems the foe will win
Seize your pride and honour.
Victory is no low fruit for easy plucking
but high and tight you must fight for it
For ever and a day hold tight
For the steadfast, for the loyal
For the faithful will overcome

Solomon Mutswairo
Zimbabwean poet

Prologue

On 15 October 2004, Morgan Tsvangirai, president of Zimbabwe's official opposition party, the Movement for Democratic Change (MDC), arrived at the imposing colonial building of the High Court in Harare.

He got out of his car, waited for his wife Susan to join him, and then, flanked by bodyguards, walked into the building.

To the cheers of his supporters he entered the court to hear what future awaited him. He was escorted into the dock where he waited patiently for Judge Paddington Garwe to hand down his judgment on the charge of treason that Tsvangirai faced. He was accused of plotting to kill President Robert Gabriel Mugabe.

Outside the court, many other Tsvangirai supporters were prevented from entering the building. Included in the throng was his personal spokesperson and assistant, William Bango. Some of the crowd began to toyi-toyi and the police took out their batons and started hitting people. Bango waited impatiently. It was to be one of the longest waits of his life.

Inside, seated in the mahogany-panelled courtroom, Tsvangirai looked around and thought of the men before him who had waited for judgment in this place. Although Tsvangirai knew that he was innocent, he had a sinking feeling that he might not be so lucky in the outcome of his trial. He knew that he might have to pay the ultimate price for his struggle against tyranny and for the return of democracy and the rule of law in Zimbabwe – he could be sentenced to death by hanging.

He briefly pondered how he had come to this place in his life. From such a simple and humble beginning, how was it that he was in the international spotlight accused of conspiracy to murder the president of his country?

His silent reverie was interrupted as the court stirred and the clerk called out for everyone to rise. Then, as Judge Garwe banged his gavel on the mahogany podium to call the court to order, Morgan Tsvangirai took a deep breath and turned to meet his fate.

1

The Early Years

Morgan Richard Tsvangirai was born into a rural peasant family on 10 March 1952, the first of nine children (seven boys and two girls). Unlike many rural children, he had the advantage of parents who believed that their son should receive the best possible education to ensure a successful future.

Like many of his generation, Morgan's father, Dzingirai Tsvangirai, had gone to South Africa where he worked for four years in the gold mines of the Witwatersrand. Apart from saving enough money to pay the lobola for his wife Lydia Zvaipa, he had learnt an important thing in the fast-moving Johannesburg of the late 1940s: the key to success was education. South Africa was transforming itself into a highly industrialised, commercial society and Southern Rhodesia had begun to follow its lead.

The country that Tsvangirai was born in was also experiencing a new spread of African nationalism. Black political groups had been active in the south of the country since before the First World War, but they were small. The early nationalist group comprised just a few urbanised Africans with formal education, mainly teachers and clerks, and a handful of clergy.

Some of these relatively affluent and educated activists had been recruited, while in South Africa, to fill supervisory and clerical posts. A relationship had developed between the newly formed African National Congress (ANC) in South Africa and educated Ndebele from western Rhodesia and Shona from the rest of the country.[1]

Dzingirai Tsvangirai was a trained bricklayer and carpenter who helped his wife to tend their crops in between his building contracts. He was almost Victorian in his strict adherence to traditional family values. Dzingirai was determined that Morgan should receive a proper education in spite of the obstacles confronting black children.

The young Morgan had a loving mother with whom he has always had, and still enjoys, a close relationship. Despite the many hardships that Lydia has endured – losing her father when she was only two or three years old, working in other people's fields so that her two younger sisters could further their education, and being divorced by Dzingirai – she has always been a role model for Morgan with her strength and unshakeable moral values.

When Dzingirai returned from working on the mines in South Africa, the Tsvangirai family settled in the village of Nerutanga. Unlike most of their neighbours who lived in mud and straw huts, Dzingirai's skill as a bricklayer meant that the Tsvangirai's homestead – a main living area, a kitchen, the boys' bedroom and a granary – was built of brick.

More than 50 years later, this homestead is still very much home to Morgan and Susan Tsvangirai and their six children. He returns each year to help plough their field with a team of oxen. In fact, Morgan believes, 'It is really important to remember where you come from if you want to know where you are going,' and he travels home whenever he can to reconnect with his rural roots.[2]

All of the Tsvangirai children had to help with the household chores and, from the age of five, Morgan and his younger brother Colin (aged four) spent time minding the handful of family cattle that grazed on communal land in the Buhera district.

Rural life was often quite carefree for the children. In wet years the land was lush and fertile. Crops grew easily and did not have to be tended by hand with water carried from the river. When it did not rain, however, life was hard and growing enough food for the family was, so Morgan describes, 'like squeezing oil out of a stone'. In drought years Lydia sometimes resorted to feeding her family with drought-resistant *mungu*, the highly nutritious sorghum that was normally used only for feeding the chickens because it was so much tougher to grind in the giant wooden pestle and mortar. Although he much preferred *sadza* – stiff porridge made from white maize, still the staple diet of most Zimbabweans – Morgan as the eldest child helped his mother with this laborious job so that they would have enough to eat.

Morgan has few childhood memories, but he does recall his father as extremely industrious: 'a good farmer, a good builder and a good family man'. His word was the last on any matter. He recalls that his parents were very attentive to him and that as the eldest son he had certain privileges. The first seven children in the Tsvangirai family were all boys and, in general, they were close and did not fight much. As the eldest, Morgan became very protective of his younger brothers and sisters and he learnt to shoulder responsibility for others from a young age.

Later in life, his parents divorced when Dzingirai took a new young wife and had a family with her. Of all the children, Morgan has perhaps stayed closest to his father, but still says that he does not understand how he could have walked out on his wife and their children. Although Morgan was employed and independent by the time that his parents got divorced, he still found it a shocking experience – divorce, especially in those days, was not common in Shona culture.

A big influence in the young Morgan's life was his maternal grandmother, Jonika Satsai Matsinde, who lived nearby. She had been widowed young, with three children. After remarrying she had another three children. She showed Morgan, her eldest grandson, a rare understanding, and he returned a deep respect for her. Her interest in him contributed to the self-confidence that grew within him into manhood.

When Morgan was old enough to go to school, he had to manage a ten-kilometre walk each way, whatever the weather. He was always barefoot and when times were hard he also frequently had to set off without breakfast.

The first school that he attended, from 1959 until 1966, was Munyira Primary in Buhera. At first he did not take easily to learning. Instead of giving up on him and taking him out of school at the end of Standard Three, like so many parents of his contemporaries, Dzingirai sent his son away to Gonese Primary School in Hwedza for Standard Four. Whether the school was much better, or the shock of being away from home and staying with relatives made him apply himself to his studies, the effect on Morgan's performance at school was dramatic.

His marks improved so much that his father decided to bring him back to Chikara Primary where Morgan found himself top of the class, in Standards Five and Six, passing with excellent results.

Towards the end of his two years at Chikara, Morgan started looking around for schools where he could further his studies. On the advice of his teachers he decided to apply to several mission schools. He found their addresses and wrote to them. The next step was to post the letters at the local post office. He walked into the post office at Buhera and asked the postmaster for some stamps. The postmaster, an elderly 'thick-necked, red-faced Afrikaner', barked back: 'What do you want stamps for?'

'I am applying for a place at senior school, sir,' was Morgan's polite reply, with the emphasis on the 'sir'.

'You shouldn't be wasting your time or money – you blacks can't learn anything!'

Fortunately, this attitude did not discourage Morgan and he stood his ground, again insisting on buying the stamps, which were grudgingly handed over.

His persistence paid off and in 1968 he managed to secure a place at Silveira, a Catholic missionary boarding school for black pupils 20 kilometres east of Harare. Here he excelled amid the 35 other pupils in his class. In particular, his English flourished: Silveira was the first school where he had to speak English all the time. Like many children from a similar background, he did not speak English at home and had never had the opportunity to meet and talk with English-speaking people.

By the time Morgan left Silveira, his love of learning was in overdrive. After some negotiating with his father, who felt that he didn't have enough money to pay for the fees, Morgan transferred to Gokomere High School in 1970. This was also a mission-based school and here he spent two further years studying for his 'O' levels. He had developed a huge interest not only in doing well in his set subjects, but also in finding out about the world.

Gokomere High School was the perfect learning environment for a young man with a deepening interest in current affairs and global politics. The school had a good library, and the boys also had access to current affairs periodicals such as *Time* and *Newsweek*. It was through these sources that Morgan gained a window on a world far beyond his rural Rhodesia.

His interest in politics had first been aroused in 1965 while at

Chikara Primary. A young teacher came into the classroom to announce that UDI (the Unilateral Declaration of Independence) had been declared by Prime Minister Ian Smith, and explained the ramifications of the Smith government's rebellion against British rule. Morgan recalls the event clearly: 'It was shortly after lunch, at about 2.30. He came into the classroom and said he had something to tell us. Prime Minister Ian Smith had declared his government's own independence from Britain. Some of the boys snickered and asked, "What does this have to do with us?" Our teacher then explained. I understood fully that Ian Smith's Rhodesian Front had stolen the true independence of our country from us – I was appalled.'

The years prior to UDI had followed a complicated and increasingly violent road as various political leaders – white and black – negotiated amongst themselves and with the United Kingdom over the country's future.

In 1957 the Southern Rhodesian African National Congress (ANC) was formed under the charismatic leadership of Joshua Nkomo. The timing for such a movement was perfect. Within a short time, the Southern Rhodesian ANC had gained mass support in both rural and urban areas where poverty and overcrowding prompted blacks to seek a movement to redress the imbalances in the lives they led. In spite of the movement's peaceful activities, Prime Minister Edgar Whitehead banned the Southern Rhodesian ANC in 1959. Several hundred members were arrested and detained without trial, including Nkomo.

In 1960, while Nkomo was still in prison, black political activists regrouped and formed the National Democratic Party (NDP). Nkomo was elected president. The leadership of this new nationalist movement, far more militant in achieving its aims than the Southern Rhodesian ANC had been, included

Ndabaningi Sithole, Robert Mugabe and Herbert Chitepo, a brilliant man who was the first black Rhodesian advocate.

Mugabe was newly returned from a teaching job in Ghana. Here he had met his future wife, Sally. Ghana, as the first African colony to achieve independence, was a political laboratory where Africans were gaining swift advancement in government, the civil service, commerce, industry and education.

In May 1960, Mugabe returned to Rhodesia and found a country in turmoil. Black nationalists demanded political power and angry crowds swelled the streets of Salisbury, the Rhodesian capital, later to be renamed Harare. The official response, other than forcefully dispersing the crowds, was the Law and Order Maintenance Act. This enabled the government to curb freedom of speech, assembly and movement, and strengthened its powers to arrest and detain anyone without trial. The Act practically turned Rhodesia into a police state.

Repression increased and the NDP was banned in December 1961. The nationalists responded by forming two rival parties: the Zimbabwe African People's Union (Zapu) headed by Joshua Nkomo, and the Zimbabwe African National Union (Zanu) led by Ndabaningi Sithole, with Mugabe as secretary-general.[3]

Demand by the white Rhodesians for immediate Dominion status had become vociferous. After lengthy discussions with Britain, a new constitution was introduced for Southern Rhodesia in December 1961 (and finally became law in November 1962). It allowed for minority African representation, but because of its limitations it was opposed by the black political leaders in Southern Rhodesia. Consequently, in September 1962 Zapu, the principal African opposition party, was banned, and its leaders subsequently placed 'under restriction', after various acts of terrorism and intimidation had allegedly occurred.

In November 1962 the governing United Federal Party under Sir Edgar Whitehead pledged an end to racism in Southern Rhodesia. This pledge probably helped to bring about the party's total defeat in the elections of December 1962, which were won by the right-wing Rhodesian Front (RF), led by Winston Field, who became prime minister of Rhodesia (as Southern Rhodesia was now known).

Field visited London to press for immediate independence for Rhodesia. Both Britain and Rhodesia had assumed that the 1961 constitution was the prelude to Rhodesian independence. Britain wished to ensure ultimate majority rule (in other words, rule by black Africans) within a specified time period, but the Rhodesian government was not prepared to countenance this.

The level of violence increased, and from mid-1962 young men began leaving the country for military and guerrilla training in various African states and Eastern Bloc countries abroad. Civil unrest broke out in the country, and the police, with the help of police reserve volunteers, were called in to quell the riots.

In April 1964, Ian Smith succeeded the indecisive Field as prime minister, and led the ultimately fruitless negotiations with the British government over the future of Rhodesia.[4] Finally, in 1965, Smith issued the Unilateral Declaration of Independence (UDI), proclaiming that Rhodesia was an independent country. During the five years from UDI until 1970, when Rhodesia declared itself a Republic, the Smith government and Harold Wilson's Labour government met several times to attempt to negotiate a settlement whereby Rhodesia's status as a crown colony or as an independent entity could be resolved. Britain continued to insist that any settlement must include eventual majority rule for the country. It also upheld the importance of ensuring that there was no oppression of the majority by the minority and vice versa. Two meetings, one held on HMS *Tiger* in December 1966, the other on HMS *Fearless* nearly two years later, came to nothing.

In March 1970, the RF won all 50 seats in a general election held that month. The government was further elated when Britain voted in a Tory government under Edward Heath. In a new initiative to settle the 'Rhodesia problem', Heath sent envoys to Salisbury to try to reach an agreement with the rebel government.

Agreement was almost forthcoming. The British delegation, under Sir Alec Douglas Home, proposed a plan that still entrenched racial segregation but introduced a larger voters' roll for black people, albeit with various educational and property qualifications. This was intended to lead to majority rule but only decades into the future. In view of the prevailing discrimination in the standards of education, Britain offered £50 million in aid for black educational development. Smith and his RF party supported the agreement although it was probably far more liberal than they would have liked.

The next step was to get the country to accept it – and this meant including Africans as well. A commission headed by Lord Pearce was given the task of gauging opinion and undertook a tour of the entire country early in 1972. Commissioners met with over 6 000 whites and more than 114 000 blacks. The total black population over the age of 18 was estimated to be nearly two million at the time. Nearly 6 per cent of the black population were thus consulted. The settlement proposal was rejected by a resounding majority of them.[5]

Behind this response was the exiled and imprisoned African nationalist leadership, who worked together to launch the African National Council on 16 December 1971 in order to fight the proposal. Heading the temporary pressure group were two Methodist ministers without prior political prominence, Abel Muzorewa and Canaan Banana.[6]

Smith had been confident of a 'yes' result, saying that Rhodesia's black people were possibly 'the happiest blacks in Africa'.[7] When the poll results were published, Smith denounced the exercise as 'an absolute fraud'.[8] After this, Britain had no option but to back off. Smith's government was seen to be unrepresentative, and Rhodesia faced its own future alone.

Thoroughly symptomatic of what lay ahead was the rapid increase in guerrilla activity and attacks on white farms. Years would go by of military conflict between the Rhodesian armed forces and nationalist guerrillas before the Lancaster House talks ended the war and finally paved the way for an independent Zimbabwe and the first democratic elections.

Within a year of the Pearce Commission, an armed offensive had opened in the north-east of Rhodesia. When fighting broke out in the Centenary area at the end of 1972, a new phase in the struggle for liberation began.[9] Chimurenga had commenced in earnest. Soon guerrillas were infiltrating into the east of the country, stretching Rhodesia's security forces still further. By 1976, 15 000 to 20 000 guerrillas were either under arms or in training, and most of these were believed to be in Mozambique.

It was against this background of political activity that Morgan Tsvangirai matured, so his interest in current affairs and politics – both local and global – was hardly surprising. By the time Morgan arrived at Gokomere High School in 1970 he was totally against everything that the Smith government stood for. His fellow students, amused by his political focus, gave him the nickname 'Arafat' because of his revolutionary ideas of freeing the country from 'the oppressor' and his deep interest in current affairs. A school friend, Robert Mawire, recalls: 'Morgan was a fiery, tough character. I remember he loved to debate and argue the political and social issues of the day.'[10]

Mawire also remembers Morgan's compassion towards other boys, particularly the younger ones, perhaps because he missed his siblings at home. Above all, Mawire recalls Morgan's positive outlook and his academic success: 'He was very charismatic and popular. I am not the slightest bit surprised that he has got to where he is today.'

After passing eight 'O' level subjects, Morgan was invited to study 'A' levels at St Ignatius, near Harare – a singular honour at the time, reserved only for the brightest and hardest-working black students with parents who could make the financial sacrifice to pay for two more years of study. Unfortunately, Morgan's father had already supported him for two years at 'O' level: 'I was desperate to do my "A" levels, but just could not ask my father to sponsor me any further. I knew my days of formal learning were over. From now I was on my own and would have to try and find a way to help with the education of my younger brothers.'

The family decided that Morgan should seek work in Umtali (now Mutare), where his father was employed by the city council as a bricklayer. Job-hunting was a depressing exercise. His classmates and teachers had appreciated him for who he was and for his burgeoning intellect. Now he was viewed as one of hundreds of young black men seeking employment. It took him a long time to find any sort of work. Employers were not looking for people with 'O' levels; at every turn he was told that he was overqualified. Eventually he found a job as a sweeper in a textile factory, Elastics & Tapes, for just $5 – five Rhodesian dollars – a week.

The job involved working shifts and was excessively tedious and routine. Although a job in textiles was not exactly what

Morgan had had in mind, he joined the Textile Workers' Union, encouraged at his workplace by a 'very fiery' trade unionist, Phineas Sithole. 'Sithole was utterly convincing. He persuaded us that joining the union was the right thing to do and so all the workers joined the union.'

Towards the end of his time in Umtali Morgan became a loom weaver. His salary went up to $15 a week – now he could buy a bed, a wardrobe, more food and 'a little drink'. However, he realised that it was not the life for him. Although he was able to contribute to his family's finances, Morgan dreamt of a job where he could use his education to advance himself.

The armed resistance struggle was gaining in intensity at this time. Many of his friends and acquaintances in Umtali had slipped across the border into Mozambique to join training camps. Although intrigued by the armed struggle and the romantic idealism of fighting against the country's racial system, Morgan had family responsibilities. He was an important potential source of income for the household and comments: 'My first priority was my responsibility to the family … I never even considered leaving [to join the war] – except for a few wistful moments.'

Despite his low wages, Morgan Tsvangirai bought newspapers to keep up with local and international affairs. One day he saw an advertisement for plant operators at the Anglo American-owned Trojan Nickel Mine in Bindura. The mine employed about 2 500 people. Praying that he would have a chance to improve his earnings and find a more interesting job, he applied along with about 700 others. He was short-listed for one of twelve positions. After an intensive interview and psychometric testing process, he was hired at the 'vast' salary of $75 a week. 'I could not believe my luck – it was a huge amount of money to me. In those days you could buy a car for $500.'

He started his training, which he found an immense challenge, writing tests to earn his certificate as an operator in the smelting plant. Apart from having to learn so many new things, he found the job physically challenging. Fortunately, he was young and strong and, above all, felt that he was achieving something to help his family and win a better life for himself. By then he was helping to pay his brothers' school fees. One of them – Casper – was thus able to complete his 'A' levels and attend university. It was fortunate that Morgan was able to improve his earnings when he did, for at around this time Dzingirai announced that he was tired of providing endlessly for his brood and handed much of the responsibility over to his eldest son.

As the bush war intensified in the late 1970s, many of the white plant operators were often away on military service. This must have been a nightmare for the management on the mine, but it also gave Morgan great scope for advancement and he rose through the ranks. As he said, 'It is ironic that the bush war, which was waged to preserve Rhodesia as a sanctuary for whites, gave me so many opportunities to advance myself.'

In 1976 he was promoted to the position of general foreman. By now, he recalls, his life was the closest he'd ever come to what he considered normal. He was 26 years old and could provide for his extended family while enjoying a good standard of living. With the promotion he moved into a three-bedroomed home in the mine compound in Bindura. It was time, he felt, to find himself a wife. One day as he walked through the compound, he saw Susan Nyaradzo for the first time. He nudged the friend who was walking next to him and said, 'That is the girl I am going to marry!'

Susan was visiting an uncle who worked for the mine. She also came from Buhera, the district of Morgan's childhood, from what he calls 'a strong family'. Once Morgan had paid his respects to her uncle and aunt, who were acting as chaperons, he was allowed to take Susan out and the two quickly realised the depth of their relationship. When she eventually went home to Buhera they started writing to each other. Their correspondence led to marriage in July 1978, after an appropriate lobola had been negotiated. The couple decided not to have a traditional wedding ceremony in case it was disrupted by either the army or Zanla guerrillas. Villages in the Buhera district were often caught in the cross-fire of military operations. It seemed best to get married in court. The first time that Morgan was ever photographed was the day after he got married when he, Susan and one of his younger brothers, Samuel, posed for a picture.

As an ardent supporter of Robert Mugabe and Zanu-PF, Tsvangirai remained opposed to the Smith government and all that it stood for, but at this point he was not involved in politics, carrying on with his job as works foreman at the Trojan Nickel Mine.

Rhodesia's road to independence and freedom was a convoluted and bloody one. In 1975, the Victoria Falls conference was held in South African railway coaches on the bridge spanning the border between Zimbabwe and Zambia. The meeting, between Ian Smith and leaders of the black nationalist movement, had been initiated by South African prime minister John Vorster.[11] These talks were aimed at working towards a constitutional conference, but they failed as Smith refused to accept the possibility of majority rule in the foreseeable future.

In mid-April 1976, a new British initiative headed by Foreign Secretary David Owen got under way with Owen visiting Rhodesia – the first cabinet member from the United Kingdom to do so in six years. Essentially he told Smith that if some sort of constitutional settlement was not reached, Rhodesia's oil supply would be cut off.

Then, in October 1976, with the bush war more bitter by the day, there was another failed attempt to settle the 'Rhodesia problem'. A conference was held in Geneva, chaired by the British ambassador to the UN, Ivor Richards. A couple of weeks prior to the Geneva conference Robert Mugabe, in exile in Maputo after spending eleven years in Rhodesian prisons, and Joshua Nkomo (who had had a similar history) had announced the formation of the Patriotic Front (PF). This new coalition of Zanu and Zapu excluded Sithole and Muzorewa. On its formation the PF was immediately endorsed as the primary nationalist body of the struggle for Zimbabwe by the 'front-line' presidents of African states bordering on Rhodesia as well as by the Liberation Committee of the OAU.

Discussions at the Geneva conference faltered over an acceptable timetable for transition to majority rule. The nationalists wanted the transition to be complete within a year, while Smith wanted twice as long to bring in a one-man, one-vote system. The conference also disagreed over office bearers in the proposed transitional government. Smith's government wanted a complicated two-tiered, multiracial council system. This was rejected out of hand by the nationalists. They also particularly resisted Smith's intention to retain control over the police and the army. The Geneva conference dragged on until December, when it was adjourned. An attempt by the British to restart it in January 1977 failed.

During all these behind-the-scenes negotiations the blistering bush war continued. The Rhodesian security forces mounted major raids into Mozambique to kill large numbers of people who they alleged were threatening the safety of the country. These were the same people the nationalists described as Rhodesian refugees and Mozambican civilians.

At the end of November 1977, Ian Smith finally announced his formal acceptance of the concept of majority rule. In April 1964, when he became prime minister of Rhodesia, he had sworn that he would never accept majority rule. His final capitulation came not a moment too soon. Smith started negotiations with the country's internal black leaders, Bishop Muzorewa, Ndabaningi Sithole and Chief Chirau, while the Patriotic Front leaders met secretly in Malta with David Owen and UN ambassador Andrew Young. Both Nkomo and Mugabe accepted the idea of independently observed elections that would end the war, but they also insisted on being part of any transitional government in the period leading up to the elections.

Finally, after delicate and fraught negotiations at Lancaster House, Zimbabwe gained its independence in 1980. Robert Mugabe became the country's first prime minister and Canaan Banana the first president.

On the eve of Zimbabwe's independence in 1980 Robert Mugabe delivered a landmark speech allaying the fears of white Zimbabweans and the international community:

> If yesterday I fought you as an enemy, today you have
> become a friend and an ally with the same national
> interest, loyalty, rights and duties as myself ... The
> wrongs of the past must now stand forgiven and
> forgotten. If we ever look to the past, let us do so for
> the lesson the past has taught us, namely that oppression
> and racism are inequalities that must never find scope in
> our political and social system. It could never be a correct
> justification that because the whites oppressed us yester-

day when they had power, the blacks must oppress them today because they have power. An evil remains an evil whether practised by white against black or black against white.[12]

Like all Zimbabweans, black and white, Tsvangirai was impressed by Mugabe's declared intent to heal the wounds of the past and move forward as leader of a united country. Indeed, he hailed Mugabe as a hero, and often says of that time: 'I would have laid down my life for him.' It would not take many years for this situation to change.

2

Uniting Trade Unionists

'A nation can win freedom without its people becoming free.'

– Joshua Nkomo[1]

At the time of Zimbabwe's independence, Morgan Tsvangirai was enjoying his new position as the works foreman at the Trojan Nickel Mine in Bindura. He was also revelling in family life with Susan and their small son, Edwin, born in 1979.

While his personal environment was peaceful and full of hope for the future, within weeks of independence a wave of industrial unrest hit Zimbabwe. An estimated 200 strikes were organised in 1980 and 1981. The major cause of the strikes was workers' low pay. Although most were short-lived, the strikes symbolised an impatience with the slow transformation in labour relations.[2] This unrest lasted for the next 18 months and was frequently met with harshness on the part of the police and government officials.[3]

In spite of, or perhaps because of, the challenges facing workers, Tsvangirai was relishing his role within the Associated Mine Workers Union. As the chairperson of the Trojan Mine branch of the union he was interested in the role that he could play in improving the lot of the miners whose interests he represented.

He found that the dual role that he held as a member of the mine's management team and as a trade unionist representing the workers allowed him unique insights into labour issues that came up for discussion. He could see each side's views with real under-standing: he knew Anglo American's perspective and was able to convey this in practical terms to the workers whom he was speak-ing for. Real progress was made in finding common ground and his negotiating skills were becoming finely honed.

In 1983, he was appointed to the national executive of the union. His position meant that he represented miners from all over the country including Matabeleland. Here a sinister drama was unfolding in the 'Gukurahundi', a Shona term that is literal-ly translated as 'the rain that washes away the chaff before the spring rains'.[4]

Like many Zimbabweans, particularly those who lived in Mashonaland, Tsvangirai knew little of what was going on in the country's south. He first became aware that something was afoot when he went to visit one of the mines in Matabeleland and heard people talking in undertones about 'dissidents'. However, the gov-ernment's propaganda campaign was so effective that it cast doubt on these rumours. Tsvangirai now comments: 'What I did not pick up at the time was the brutality of the security forces against the people. I believe that we are guilty of sins of omission.'

The Gukurahundi of the early 1980s was the first wave of genocide against the Ndebele, carried out by a special military unit, the Fifth Brigade, whose formation had been instigated by Robert Mugabe within months of his taking office.[5] The Korean-trained Fifth Brigade struck fear into the hearts of the Ndebele as they tortured, raped and murdered people with impunity. The government explained away these atrocities as the work of 'dissidents'.

While some acts of violence were undoubtedly committed by Zanla and Zipra (the military wings of Zanu and Zapu respectively) ex-combatants, and South Africa's apartheid government had to a degree been involved in attempts to destabilise Zimbabwe, there were, in reality, two overlapping conflicts in Matabeleland. The first was between the dissidents and government defence units, which included the Fourth Brigade, Sixth Brigade, the Paratroopers, the Central Intelligence Organisation (CIO), and the Police Support Unit. However, the majority of atrocities were the result of a second conflict that involved government agencies (primarily the Fifth Brigade, the CIO, the Police Internal Security Intelligence Unit or PISI, and the Zanu-PF youth brigades) and all those who were alleged to support Zapu.[6]

By 1983, the country was tense. Joshua Nkomo was being constantly harassed and, in fear of his life, fled into exile in Botswana. He returned in 1985, just in time for the March election – to avoid losing his seat in parliament – and eventually negotiated the Unity Pact, which was signed between Zanu-PF and Zapu at the end of 1987. This pact is seen by most Ndebele-speakers as the inevitable capitulation by Zapu's Nkomo, who had watched the drastic results of the government's Gukurahundi campaign. The agreement between the parties made Zanu-PF's pre-eminent position in the 'new' party quite clear and set the stage for the government's increasing repression of any opposition.

The government's propaganda campaign proved effective and many people, Morgan Tsvangirai included, never knew the truth of what was really happening to the Ndebele until years later. The truth behind the killings was revealed to the world by Peter Godwin, the Zimbabwean-born, British journalist turned author, who shocked the world in a London *Sunday Times* exposé entitled 'Mass Murder in Matabeleland: The Evidence'.[7]

All told, the Gukurahundi claimed at least 20 000 lives between 1982 and 1988, and many more people simply disappeared.[8] Nearly everyone in Matabeleland was affected in some way and among these people were the miners in whom Tsvangirai had an active interest.

In 1985, after ten years' service on the mine, Tsvangirai resigned and moved his family to Harare to take up a full-time post as the vice-president of the Associated Mine Workers Union of Zimbabwe. It was a big step. He was leaving a lucrative job with excellent security and prospects to move into the union movement on a full-time basis. He felt that he could contribute to the union movement's effort to protect and promote the rights of miners in Zimbabwe. In 1985, Zimbabwe's mining industry was thriving. Gold, coal, nickel, asbestos, iron and chrome all contributed to Zimbabwe's strong economy. One Zimbabwean dollar could be exchanged for one United States dollar, and the country was a major player in Africa.

It was also around this time that Tsvangirai's disillusionment with Zanu-PF and Mugabe set in. Like many others, Tsvangirai had hoped that the position of workers would improve under a Zanu-PF government, but from the evidence of the first three years of independence it was apparent that the workers' situation was actually worsening. Initially, the Zanu-PF government espoused a socialist stance that coincided with Tsvangirai's perspectives. However, the ruling party failed to implement socialist policies and the trade unions became increasingly impatient and disillusioned.[9]

Tsvangirai threw himself into his new career and soon earned a reputation as a person who got things done. On one occasion there was an industrial dispute at one of the mines that was not being attended to because there was no transport for the union officials – their vehicle was in the garage for repairs. When Tsvangirai heard about the problem he did not hesitate. He hopped onto one of the Shu Shine buses – rather unreliable, ancient buses cheerily clad in Shu Shine advertisements – that service the more remote areas of Zimbabwe. These buses are known for stopping at every village and road intersection, taking passengers forever to get to their destinations. In this way, Morgan travelled to the mine, stayed overnight to sort out the problem, and returned to Harare the next day via the Shu Shine express.[10]

Tsvangirai's new boss at the Associated Mine Workers Union was Jeffrey Mutandare, who was also the head of the Zimbabwe Congress of Trade Unions (ZCTU). The ZCTU had been formed in 1981, with Albert Mugabe (Robert's brother) as its first secretary-general. This new body served to amalgamate most of Zimbabwe's trade unions. At that stage, Zanu-PF was pursuing a Marxist-Leninist ideology and saw a powerful but subservient trade union movement as an asset in its fight against what it perceived as a capitalist system left over from Rhodesia's days as a British colony.

In mid-1988 Tsvangirai joined the ZCTU as its secretary-general. Six months later, Mutandare was investigated, prosecuted and convicted of defrauding an American labour organisation.[11] He was jailed for an effective six months and was forced to resign as president of the ZCTU.

Gibson Sibanda, vice-president of the MDC, succeeded Mutandare, and so began the extremely productive working relationship between Sibanda and Tsvangirai that was to see them unite Zimbabwean workers and form a powerful informal opposition to Mugabe's government. The pair of them undertook to professionalise the union and stamp out the corruption that had plagued it. Their success in these endeavours is borne out by the support that they received from the International Confederation of Free Trade Unions, based in Brussels, as well as by the fact that at its height ZCTU had more than 360 000 members.[12] (At the time of writing, Zimbabwe's serious economic woes and major unemployment had caused this figure to slump to less than 170 000 members.)[13]

Tsvangirai and Sibanda restructured the ZCTU into eight departments, including an information resource centre that published *The Worker* to communicate with workers. This was especially important in the context of the media being largely government-owned.

Shortly after his appointment as secretary-general of the ZCTU, Tsvangirai drafted a five-year development plan for the union. It outlined the union's goals: increasing administrative efficiency; the mobilisation of workers to participate fully in the activities of their individual unions; and, most important of all, the complete overhaul and restructuring of the labour movement in Zimbabwe.

This document is also interesting for the insight that it provides into Tsvangirai's thinking at the time. He recalls that there was a period when he flirted quite intentionally with Marxist ideology: 'It was a temptation, for it was the current political thinking. I visited the Soviet Union in 1986 with a labour delegation as part of an exchange programme. There were some positive aspects to Marxism, but it was all too regimented for my comfort. I didn't like the class distinction – not among employers, workers and managers but between the ruling élite and the rest of the population. This is very much the case in Zimbabwe, except here the small ruling élite has acquired power and wealth for themselves at the expense of everyone – they profess to pursue Marxist policies while they do not even follow socialist ones.'

Although Tsvangirai still has the worker's interests at heart, his ideology and rhetoric have matured to the point where he has become a dedicated social democrat who can think laterally enough to harness all that a capitalist-driven economy can offer while constantly keeping in mind the upliftment of the poor. In July 2002 he elaborated on this perspective: 'You need to create a platform of reward for individual initiatives because, without that reward, there is no motivation. At the end of the day you need to have a society that also has a social conscience. What we have got is a ruling party that has even betrayed the principles of African fairness. The ruling élite has seriously betrayed the ideals of the liberation struggle.'

From the outset of his time as secretary-general of the ZCTU, Tsvangirai strove to distance and disentangle the union from Zanu-PF. 'We knew we had to become autonomous from government and to make the union financially viable,' he says. 'The moment we started protesting to the government over the plight of workers – that is when the trouble began.'

In his first major battle with government, Tsvangirai remonstrated over the continued detention of University of Zimbabwe students protesting against government corruption. He found himself arrested and detained under state of emergency regulations on allegations of being a spy for South Africa.

It was a worrying time for Tsvangirai. At first he was moved from holding cell to holding cell, not able to receive visits from his lawyer or wife and not being given anything to read. Eventually Susan was allowed to visit him. He was imprisoned for six weeks, but not charged. Ultimately he was freed by the courts – only to be imprisoned again.

When he was first detained, the International Confederation of Free Trade Unions sent a young Zambian union leader to plead for Tsvangirai. The Zimbabwe government responded by detaining and deporting him. Two years later that labour leader, Frederick Chiluba, became Zambia's democratically-elected president defeating Kenneth Kaunda after decades of one-party rule.

This incident marked the first of many times that Tsvangirai crossed swords with Robert Mugabe's Zanu-PF. Between 1989 and 2004, Tsvangirai was to be arrested, imprisoned or brought in for questioning countless times.

After his release from prison, Tsvangirai moved away completely from the ruling party and became openly critical of its activities. He became recognised as one of the few voices in Zimbabwe that could stand up to Mugabe.[14]

The ZCTU became openly defiant of Mugabe, at one point heckling him at May Day celebrations, which he addressed every year. The widening rift between the ZCTU and Mugabe eventually forced the president to cancel his traditional addresses at such meetings.[15]

Mugabe also faced opposition from other sources. In 1988, Edgar Tekere, a Zanu-PF stalwart and close friend of Mugabe, had been expelled from Zanu-PF for openly criticising the party, citing corruption and mismanagement and calling for the party leadership to be comprehensively reformed. Tekere responded to his expulsion by forming a new political party, the Zimbabwe Unity Movement (ZUM). In the 1990 parliamentary and presidential elections, despite its members being harassed and subject to political violence, Tekere's ZUM captured two seats and nearly 20 per cent of the total vote.

In addition, 1990 saw the lapse of the government's emergency powers just prior to the meeting of the Harare Commonwealth Conference. This was to have a marked effect on the relationship between the government and workers. The decade

1990 to 2000 saw a widening of democratic space as civil society took advantage of a Bill of Rights that had become fully effective for the first time in the country's history.[16]

In 1991 a further wedge was driven between the labour movement and the government with the formal introduction of Zimbabwe's Economic Structural Adjustment Programme (Esap). Dubbed by ordinary Zimbabweans as the 'Extra Suffering for the African People', Esap was an economic programme motivated by the World Bank, which said that it would not lend money to Zimbabwe unless the country instituted economic reforms and adopted free-market principles.

The ZCTU repeatedly called for dialogue with the government on Esap, which it claimed was introduced without due consultation with the labour movement. Rising prices, a shift towards contract employment, shortages and unaffordable costs of basic goods, as well as monopolistic control of the economy and the stifling of new indigenous business, were just a few of the ZCTU's concerns around Esap. On May Day 1991, President Mugabe had agreed that his government needed to confer with the unions but subsequently he remained totally inaccessible to the labour movement.[17]

From the outset Tsvangirai was critical of Esap. Not knowing how prophetic his words were to be, he is quoted as saying in 1991:

What we are looking for in Zimbabwe is democratic space. Because what is going to be sacrificed in this programme [Esap] is democracy. When people go to the streets, complaining about these things, the state will be forced to use power to quell these riots, and in fact one of the ironies is that we are arming our own people –

the police and the army – to turn against our people …
At the end of the day we become the marginalised group,
because the government has put itself in a position so
that it cannot take a stand against the IMF [International
Monetary Fund]. The only way to defend against international capital marginalising further the indigenous
businessman, the worker, the peasant, is to have all these
groups together.[18]

Prior to Esap, Zimbabwe had largely adhered to the Rhodesian-
era regulatory controls on prices and foreign trade. While these
controls restricted Zimbabwean access to foreign currency, the
country was growing reasonably steadily with the manufacturing
industry being in a healthy state, or at least maintaining its *status
quo*. Although there were economic wrongs that needed righting,
Esap forced the economy ahead of itself – Zimbabwe arguably was
not ready for global competition. The introduction of Esap, with
these curbs no longer in place, saw money being drained from the
country, with an immediate and unprecedented increase in interest
rates and inflation. In late 1991 the stock market lost 65 per cent
of its value. The drought in 1992 did not help matters. Lower agricultural productivity for many meant lower disposable incomes.

These combined factors contributed to a dramatic decrease in
manufacturing output. By 1999, the textile industry's capacity
had fallen by 64 per cent since 1980.[19] From being a major player in the African textile market, Zimbabwe became little more
than a re-export platform for South and East Asian textiles and a
dumping ground for second-hand European clothes.

When the World Bank graded Zimbabwe's adoption of Esap
as 'highly satisfactory', Tsvangirai and his colleagues were incredu-
lous. It seemed to them that the poor were becoming poorer

while certain key players in the government and industry were prospering.

Consequently, in May 1992, the ZCTU leadership, following extensive discussions with Zimbabwean workers, resolved to hold a peaceful demonstration on 13 June. Their intention was to pressurise the government into discussing matters of concern with the ZCTU. The police were approached for permission to hold the labour demonstrations, but this was denied. The ZCTU then appealed to the Supreme Court, which ruled that the police did not have the right to ban peaceful demonstrations.

However much people protested, the country's economy was starting to slide alarmingly. The price of basic foodstuffs sharply increased and, in 1993, riots over the price of bread broke out in Harare. Police were called in to quell the disturbances. Mugabe's government, in a pattern that was to be repeated, simply blamed the millers and bakers for the bread price increases. However, civic organisations unanimously pointed to Esap as the cause of the worsening social and economic conditions of Zimbabweans.

In 1994 the poverty datum line was calculated to be Z$1 200 a month for a family of four. Subsidies on basic commodities and social services, such as education and health, were removed, causing further hardship.[20] Every employee was far poorer than he or she had been in 1985. Miners found themselves earning almost 80 per cent less in real terms than they had nine years earlier, while employees in the finance sector were the hardest hit. They were, in real terms, earning only 5 per cent of what they had been bringing home in 1985.[21]

Tsvangirai was well in touch with the struggle of workers to feed, clothe, and educate their families. His own family had suddenly grown with the addition of twins – a boy and a girl – named Vincent and Millicent. Edwin, Garikai, Vimbai and Rumbidzai had been born at two-yearly intervals. However delighted the family was with the new arrivals, his expanded family made Tsvangirai wonder how people less fortunate managed to cope.

Apart from the ZCTU's battles with the government over Esap, Tsvangirai had some serious issues to confront within the confines of the union. It was cash-strapped and, instead of being able to survive on membership subscriptions, the ZCTU was forced to supplement its running costs with funds from external donors. This was something that Tsvangirai deemed 'an unhealthy situation' although it was conducted in a transparent manner.[22] To aggravate matters, the media was highlighting this situation. Jeffrey Mutandare, out of prison and now the leader of the Associated Mine Workers Union, was particularly vocal in his criticism.

Tsvangirai resolved that the way to rectify the situation was for the ZCTU to embark on a membership drive and reduce the number of affiliates from the current 35 unions to 15 through mergers and integrations. He also planned to increase subscriptions. However successful he was at professionalising the ZCTU, money always proved to be an elusive commodity. Although the union was far bigger and far more efficient when he resigned in 1999, it still had a problem getting affiliate unions to pay their subscriptions.

Tsvangirai was to clash again with Mutandare, who criticised him for the 'lack of unity and purpose between the ZCTU and the government to indigenise the economy'.[23] Tsvangirai responded by describing Mutandare as 'a player who has been shown a red card; he fumed on the terraces at both the players and the referee'.[24] He went on to explain the progress that the ZCTU had made in serving the interests of its members and Zimbabwean workers in general: it had become autonomous of the government and was now able to arrive at its own policies from an independent position; it had concluded the implementation of a social security package for all workers in the country; it had put together a comprehensive health and safety programme; it had become active in the promotion of gender-related issues; and it had established a projects department to assist those retrenched as a result of Esap to establish themselves in self-employment micro projects.

Despite these accomplishments, the ZCTU had to acknowledge that its policy of confrontation with the government over Esap had not worked. It was futile to keep protesting about Esap's failure to improve the country's economic standing. Instead, the ZCTU needed to gather documented proof over and above the simple observation that Esap was decimating Zimbabweans' lives and future prospects. Consequently, in 1995, the ZCTU commissioned a study calling in experts from various fields to provide proof that Esap was an unmitigated disaster and unsuitable for Zimbabwe's economic make-up.

The 1996 publication 'Beyond Esap' assessed the appropriateness of Esap to the developmental objectives of Zimbabwe. In the foreword Tsvangirai wrote:

> While acknowledging that SAPs [Structural Adjustment
> Programmes] are necessary, the study shows that they are
> insufficient in fostering development (that is, growth
> with equity). Zimbabwe's economy is characterized by
> a number of structural rigidities such as unequal access
> to land and finance, whilst a large proportion of its
> population is engaged in [the] informal sector. It is the
> contention of the report that under such conditions,
> there is nothing inherent in ESAP policies that will lead

to development. In fact, reliance on market forces in such
an economy, as demanded by the current policies, may
only serve to perpetuate such distortions.

'Beyond Esap' was characterised by its 'concessionary lan-
guage' and 'neoliberal policy suggestions',[25] but at this stage the
ZCTU was still attempting to avoid overt confrontation with
the government. Rather, it hoped to find a middle road that
would see a consensus being reached between workers, employers
and government. Instead, as Tsvangirai commented: ' "Beyond
Esap" really led to the labour movement being lambasted as the
government sought to suppress any expressions against the programme.'

In the face of the government's continued inaction over its
economic policy, unions staged a series of strikes at national and
industrial level. The biggest of these was an eight-week public
service strike in 1996. This was followed by a two-month health
strike. The government dealt with this strike, not as a labour dispute, but as a political challenge, and about 2 000 nurses and 200
doctors were fired.

The end of 1997 marked a turning-point in the career of
Morgan Tsvangirai. As secretary-general of the ZCTU, he became
involved in the protest against the government's latest round of
tax increases, designed to help pay the Z$4 billion compensation
for war veterans – as well as increased sales tax and a 5 per cent
war veterans' levy to be paid by all taxpayers from April 1998. The
strike was planned for 10 and 11 December 1997.

When the tax strike began on 10 December, it proved to be
the most comprehensive strike in the country's history, paralysing
the activities of the government and private sector around the
country. What had been intended as a peaceful two-day protest

was transformed into violent action after riot police attacked workers in Harare with teargas and clubs. Fearing further reprisals against the ZCTU members, Tsvangirai called off the protest after the first day, which had seen 150 000 workers around the country participate in the action.

On the morning of 11 December, Morgan Tsvangirai paid dearly for his leadership in the strike when he was attacked in his office. Eight men charged past Tsvangirai's secretary, Edith Munyaka, into his office. She followed them in and saw the men trying to push Tsvangirai, who was covered in blood from an injury to his head, out of his tenth-floor office window. The men shouted at her to get out and shoved her through the door. She screamed for help and the men fled, leaving Tsvangirai lying on the floor unconscious in a pool of blood.

Tsvangirai went for treatment at the private Avenues Clinic where he was discharged after his head was stitched up. The eight attackers, who at the time were thought to be personnel of Zanu-PF's national headquarters in Harare, were apparently later seen in a nearby bar. Tsvangirai now believes that the men were cohorts of Chenjerai 'Hitler' Hunzvi, the self-styled war veteran who was appointed in 1999 to galvanise war veterans and the Zanu-PF youth militia to take part in the politically motivated land-grab of white-owned commercial farms in the run-up to the June 2000 parliamentary elections.

Despite Tsvangirai's positive identification of one of his assailants in a police identification parade, the state ultimately refused to convict the man due to a supposed lack of evidence. Tsvangirai and his family were badly shaken by the attack but, if anything, it strengthened his resolve to keep fighting the government on the economic issues facing all Zimbabweans. Alongside Gibson Sibanda, with whom he had forged a close bond, he continued trying to engage the government in dialogue, only to be largely ignored.

In 1997 Tsvangirai started dealing closely with David Coltart, a Bulawayo lawyer who since the early 1980s had dedicated himself to human rights issues. Tsvangirai asked Coltart to speak to trade union leaders on various issues, and their relationship of mutual respect developed from there. In an interview in July 2001 Coltart commented: 'The one thing I have observed in Morgan Tsvangirai is that he does not have one drop of racist blood in his veins. Like [Nelson] Mandela he has a vision of a rainbow nation for Zimbabwe ... He also has an amazing intellect and is generally someone who remains unflustered under pressure.'

He continued: 'Morgan Tsvangirai was pivotal in the establishment of the National Constitutional Assembly in 1998, which in effect became the nursery for the establishment of the MDC the following year.'

The origins of the National Constitutional Assembly (NCA) go back to 1996. Just as the ZCTU had seen the need for constitutional change in the country, so the churches were simultaneously campaigning for a new constitution.

Recalls Tsvangirai, 'We decided to get together and coordinate our efforts into one national movement. The idea was that the constitution was faulty and was the reason why the trade union movement had found the obstacles put in their path insurmountable. We had to rework the whole constitutional framework to the development of proper trade union rights. At the same time the churches were talking about the writing of a new constitution because of the poor state of human rights in Zimbabwe. It was this convergence that brought us together into one constitutional movement.'

The various stakeholders in this new civic movement held several meetings to discuss the way forward. Lovemore Madhuku, a respected constitutional law professor at the University of Zimbabwe, was a task-force member who represented the FES (Friedrich Ebert Stiftung) in Harare, a non-governmental organisation (NGO) that supports democratic institutions. Madhuku says of Tsvangirai: 'From the first he appreciated the project, and I think that is a sign of his striking intelligence that he could grasp the potential of what we were trying to achieve. There was nothing similar around at the time, but the idea of an allied civic organisation gripped his imagination and he could immediately see its potential.'[26]

Finally, on 31 January 1998 a convention was held at which the NCA was formally launched and Morgan Tsvangirai was elected as its first chairperson.

The process leading to the formation of the NCA happened in parallel with the ZCTU's growing disillusionment with Robert Mugabe and its concern over the worsening economic plight of its members. The union continued to press for a meeting to discuss possible solutions with the country's recalcitrant president. Gibson Sibanda recollects that they had called for more than a dozen meetings with Mugabe. All of these appointments were confirmed by his office, but never took place. Eventually the parties did meet and it was decided to establish a forum to discuss and resolve pressing issues. The only drawback was that Mugabe appointed himself as chairperson of this body, with the power to veto any decision. It was inevitable that the ZCTU should quickly withdraw from active participation in the National Economic Consultative Forum.

From the outset 1999 was a momentous year. The labour movement seemed determined to enter the new millennium with a new purpose – to be heard. In fact, all sectors of Zimbabwean society seemed to be busy mobilising against the government.

One of the most important events was the establishment of the *Daily News*, the first privately-owned national daily newspaper since *The Daily Gazette* in the early 1990s.[27] At last there was an alternative to state-owned newspapers such as *The Herald* and *The Chronicle*.

The newspaper lost little time in reporting on the growing wave of corruption on the part of the ruling élite. The ZCTU had reported that since 1997, Zimbabweans had lost some Z$20 billion due to corruption. By early 2000, this figure had grown to Z$33 billion. This was one of the issues supposedly tackled by the ineffective National Economic Consultative Forum.

In the light of this, in February 1999 the ZCTU held a special congress attended by civic and human rights organisations. The purpose of the congress was to establish that there was a crisis in governance and that there needed to be an alternative political movement of the people. On 1 March, Tsvangirai announced that the federation of trade unions had 'mandated the creation of a political formation in the interests of workers'.

The new party, as Tsvangirai announced at the time, would 'challenge President Robert Mugabe's ruling Zanu-PF at next year's parliamentary elections'. The country was, he said, facing a crisis in governance, in the economy, in its constitution and a 'crisis of military intervention', internally and externally.

Tsvangirai said that the new party would not only represent labour, but also be a broad-based movement for governmental and constitutional reform. He said that there were no coherent answers from ministers on policy and he feared that all resources of the state, including the CIO, would be deployed against mounting dissent: 'We are all in this boat and we have got a drunk captain whose only place is as a museum piece,' he commented.[28]

Before the party was formally set up, the embryonic MDC began negotiations with the NCA. Tsvangirai and others also travelled across Zimbabwe gauging public opinion and collecting information. 'Only when we could see quite clearly that the people desperately needed a political alternative did we take their mandate to the next stage and launch the MDC,' Tsvangirai said in 2004.

The MDC was formally launched, to massive public acclaim as well as concern on the part of government in September 1999, at a rally at Rufaro stadium in Harare where Zimbabwe's independence celebrations had been held in 1980. Tsvangirai then resigned as chairperson of the NCA to take over his new role as president of the MDC, and to focus on preparing the party for the upcoming 2000 parliamentary elections.

3

Viva Democracy

The length of time of oppression depends on the oppressed.

– Chief Albert Luthuli[1]

Since Zanu-PF assumed power in 1980, Zimbabwe had seen the emergence of several opposition parties – but none had come close to being a serious challenge to the ruling party before the formation of the MDC.

Once the MDC was launched, and after lengthy discussions with the ZCTU president, Gibson Sibanda, it was decided to acknowledge the country's ethnic sensibilities. Morgan Tsvangirai, as a Shona, would take the helm of the MDC, and Sibanda, representing the aspirations of the Ndebele, would back him up as vice-president.

One of the things that made the MDC different from other opposition parties was that it had a strong support base and was able to build on 'the ZCTU's success with the series of effective strikes they had stage-managed since 1986'.[2]

The MDC's first order of business was to galvanise support for a 'no' vote in the upcoming referendum that Mugabe had organised. He was seeking approval for a new Zimbabwean constitution drawn up by the 395-member Constitutional Commission that was answerable to him alone. Amongst other things, the draft document prepared by this commission proposed that, in future, a president of Zimbabwe could only serve two terms of office of five years each. The only person exempt from this provision was Mugabe himself, who would be allowed to serve a further two terms as president. In addition, on receiving a copy of the draft, Mugabe inserted an amendment allowing land expropriation without consultation. This addition also decreed that Britain, and not Zimbabwe, would be responsible for paying compensation to farmers for the land seized.[3] Under the Lancaster House agreement, Britain had agreed to assist the land resettlement programme and to rally the international donor community to help.

Between 1980 and 1985 the United Kingdom provided £47 million for land reform up until 1988. Only £3 million was unspent. A report that evaluated land resettlement issues was compiled in 1988 and sent to the Zimbabwe government by the UK's Overseas Development Administration (ODA). It received no response. The UK then sought proposals from the Zimbabwe government on spending the remaining balance. A further technical mission by the ODA in 1996 resulted in new proposals for UK support for land reform. The Zimbabwe government responded towards the end of 1996, but no agreement was reached before the UK general election in May 1997.

In September 1998, with UK encouragement, the Zimbabwe government hosted a Land Conference in Harare, involving all major international donors and the multilateral institutions. Issues raised in the ODA's 1996 report were considered at the conference. The UK participated constructively and endorsed the basic principles for land reform agreed at the conference, as did the Zimbabwe government. Those principles included the need for transparency, respect for the rule of law, poverty reduction, affordability, and consistency with Zimbabwe's wider economic interests.

The 1998 conference agreed on a two-year inception phase, during which government resettlement schemes would be tried alongside ideas from the private sector and civil society. In May 1999 consultants began work to identify ways in which the UK government could provide further support for land reform in Zimbabwe. Terms of reference for a follow-up visit were agreed with the Zimbabwe government in September 1999. However, work on UK support for land reform in Zimbabwe was interrupted by the illegal farm occupations and subsequent violence in the run-up to the 2000 parliamentary elections.[4]

Despite Britain's willingness to participate in assisting the agricultural economy to grow further, Mugabe blamed the UK for the fact that the lion's share of Zimbabwe's most productive and richest commercial farms still lay in the hands of whites.

When it finally came to the referendum, the people of Zimbabwe gave Mugabe their unequivocal answer when they vetoed the draft constitution. In what can best be described as a shocking wake-up call for Zanu-PF, 55 per cent of the voters said 'no' to the adoption of the draft constitution. As the eyes of Zimbabwe, and indeed of the world, focused on Mugabe for his reaction, he had no choice but to declare publicly that he would accept the will of the people.

The newly-formed MDC was jubilant. Despite the many obstacles that the party could face, the outcome of the referendum was taken as a positive indication that it could possibly win a parliamentary election. It would be a tall order. Mugabe's presidential powers allowed him to appoint 30 MPs. Consequently, to be certain of victory, the MDC would have to win at least 76 seats – 64 per cent of the 120 to be decided by the election.[5]

However, for the first time since independence Zanu-PF faced serious and highly organised opposition.[6] As well as having the support of urbanised workers, the MDC also had the backing of the affluent white community. This included the white farmers, with their perceived influence over hundreds of thousands of farm labourers, as well as the urban white population.

Given the support that the MDC enjoyed in urban centres and amongst the white population, Zanu-PF's best chance of winning the June 2000 parliamentary elections was to capture the rural vote, including that of the farm workers, and to create a climate of hostility against Zimbabwe's white population. To this end, within months of the formation of the MDC, Mugabe announced that he was to commence a comprehensive land distribution programme and planned to seize white commercial farms to give to the 'landless poor'.

For years many rural black people had been living on overcrowded communal land. The promise of highly productive, fertile land, which for years had been giving white farmers a more-than-comfortable life-style, was irresistible. At the same time, Mugabe sought to placate the dissatisfied war veterans by giving land to them. As chairman of the war veterans Chenjerai 'Hitler' Hunzvi led this land-grab campaign, using whatever force he deemed necessary with impurity.

By March 2000, the land programme was under way with many rural peasants as well as a few urban blacks arriving on white-owned farms in order to stake their claims. Efforts to resist the invaders were met with brutality – against the farmers and their workers. In many instances the police refused to intervene. The first time they came to the aid of white farmers was on

22 April 2000 when they rescued farmer Ian Miller and his manager, Keith McGraw, who had been frog-marched to their workers' village and interrogated about their political views. Eight police officers moved in and escorted the two men back to their homestead.[7] Up until that point, more than a thousand farms had been illegally occupied.[8]

While Tsvangirai agreed that there needed to be 'a programme of land reform', he argued strongly that this reform should be 'orderly' and should 'not destabilise the economy'.[9] On 1 April 2000, the MDC and NCA arranged a peace march in Harare. Supporters from all races and walks of life gathered amidst a police presence and then held a peaceful march. Two hours into the demonstration, a mob of heavily armed war veterans ambushed the marchers, targeting the whites. They were reportedly assisted by many of the police, who fired teargas at the fleeing NCA and MDC supporters.

Towards the end of April, southern African leaders expressed their support for Robert Mugabe's land reform programme at a regional summit meeting held at Victoria Falls. South African President Thabo Mbeki called on foreign donors to fund Zimbabwe's land reform programme while the leaders of Namibia and Mozambique publicly supported Mbeki's views. There was no condemnation of the illegal occupation of farmland, and there was also no criticism of the political violence sweeping the country.[10]

As the MDC stepped up its election campaign for the June parliamentary election, incidents of violence, and even murder, against its followers became commonplace.[11] The suffering and sacrifices of MDC supporters were brought home to Morgan Tsvangirai when his polling agent, Tichaona Chimenya, and Chimenya's assistant, Talent Mabika, were killed while campaigning in Tsvangirai's home district and constituency of Buhera. Their vehicle was set on fire and they were burnt alive. The news of their deaths was a terrible blow and Tsvangirai recalls that it was perhaps at this point that he understood his opponents would do anything to prevent him from winning a seat in his home district.

He was appalled at the attacks on his party's supporters and warned that the MDC would retaliate: 'We will take violence to the doorsteps of those responsible for violence against MDC supporters ... Some of the ministers and members of parliament actually condone the violence and say that killing people is the right thing to do. From the vice-president to some of the members of parliament, we know who is involved.'[12]

Towards the end of April, under the leadership of the Commercial Farmers' Union (CFU), farmers struck a deal with the squatters occupying well over a thousand white-owned farms. This agreement allowed the occupiers to stay on the land in return for a pledge not to use violence. The two sides agreed that the occupations would stand while proper details of a scheme to resettle squatters were laid out.[13]

Tsvangirai was upset by the deal, saying, 'I think the farmers are wrong in negotiating with an outlaw ['Hitler' Hunzvi], in negotiating with a man who is causing so much suffering in those communities.'[14]

A short while afterwards, the CFU's conciliatory efforts in negotiating with Hunzvi and the war veterans – many of whom were not old enough to have seen action in the liberation struggle – were proven to be wasted. Farm occupations continued and, by the end of the first week in May, another 40 farms had been occupied. This brought the total number to 1 200. Despite Hunzvi's agreement with the CFU to stop the violence, he told a rally in Harare that the British were ruthless, cunning people and that his followers should 'seek out British passport holders and force them to leave Zimbabwe'.[15]

From the moment the land invasions began, Zimbabwe's tourism industry inevitably began to suffer and falter. In the run-up to the June 2000 parliamentary election there was a drastic decline in the arrival of foreign tourists. The resulting diminishing pools of foreign exchange, together with plunging agricultural, mining and industrial exports, marked the beginning of Zimbabwe's tumbling currency woes and galloping inflation. With fewer farmers being able to plant crops such as maize and wheat, the government had to import commodities that were far more expensive than could be produced locally.

In May 2000 Alan Dunn, an MDC regional organiser, had died a day after being brutally assaulted on his farm at Beatrice, 60 kilometres south-west of Harare. In commenting on this murder, David Coltart, the MDC's Secretary for Legal Affairs, now the Shadow Minister of Justice, said:

> What is happening is not chaos: it is carefully orchestrated: it is state-organised violence. The violence has little to do with land, legitimate issue though this is – the violence is about the destruction of the first real threat to Zanu-PF in 20 years, the MDC. The violence must be put in [the] context of President Mugabe's threat, made at the opening of the Pungwe Water Project several weeks ago, that opponents would face death and that white farmers were 'enemies of the state'. The violence is the direct result of these statements.[16]

The MDC was so appalled at the number of attacks against its supporters that the party briefly considered boycotting the elections. However, as Tsvangirai said at the time: 'We owe it to all our supporters, many of whom have suffered, to see this struggle through to its final conclusion.'[17]

It was becoming increasingly clear that there was no free and fair electoral climate for the voters of Zimbabwe. This was attested to by the disruption of the MDC's peace rallies, the farm occupations and accompanying violence as well as the government's threats to strip British descendants of their Zimbabwe citizenship, making them ineligible to vote. The government also did not issue receipts to people registering to vote – without these, how could there be an accurate administration of the voters' roll?

In addition, Zanu-PF refused to let the MDC have a copy of the voters' roll within the requisite number of days ahead of the election. The minimum time period for this is 90 days, yet the public was given access to the roll on 1 June – only to find it a mess, with the names of countless deceased people included.[18]

Another problem facing the MDC was the government decision to delimit the electoral boundaries. The boundaries in certain MDC urban strongholds had been significantly altered to include surrounding rural constituencies, which enjoyed Zanu-PF support.[19]

Then Mugabe announced the dates of the election, 24 and 25 June, before the final delimitation report had been released. The government also required that participant parties had to nominate their candidates from among voters registered on the roll by 29 May – yet the electoral roll had not been made available for inspection. Consequently, it was impossible for opposition parties to nominate candidates or mount a challenge if the candidates were not included on the voters' roll.[20]

Meanwhile, foreign election observers had arrived in Zimbabwe. It was not long before they found themselves on the wrong side of Zanu-PF supporters. Phil Matsheza, executive director of the Human Rights Research and Documentation Trust of Southern Africa, said at the end of May 2000: 'The pre-election monitoring has to start now, but we have places that are no-go areas. We have already had some of our monitors beaten up and this impinges on the whole process of pre-election monitoring.'

Despite evidence to the contrary, South Africa's President Thabo Mbeki dismissed the verdict of one United States-based observer group that said conditions would make a free and fair election impossible.[21] Mbeki's continued refusal to remonstrate with Robert Mugabe now began to elicit much comment in the South African press. For just how long was he going to avoid dealing with the realities of Zimbabwe? Now, just before the 2000 Zimbabwean parliamentary elections, it looked as though he would contribute nothing to avert disaster in the country.

Whatever Mbeki's perceived shortcomings, he was actually attempting to find a solution to the Zimbabwean land problem. He managed to persuade Saudi Arabia and the Nordic countries to put up R100 million to buy 118 commercial farms owned by whites for redistribution to landless black Zimbabweans.[22]

However, according to the BBC, a Zanu-PF spokesperson said that Mbeki's scheme marked a return to plans drawn up in 1998. These 118 farms were the same ones that Britain had agreed to finance in 1998, but had not implemented, questioning Mugabe's land distribution methods. The spokesperson said the government would not be distracted from pressing ahead with its own plans to redistribute white-owned farmland.[23]

Two weeks before the election, Mugabe stepped up his land-grab election strategy, telling Zanu-PF candidates that the nation should be grateful to the invading war veterans. 'If white farmers keep land in the future it would be out of charity and not as a legacy of colonialism,' Mugabe warned, and said that all white-owned farms could be taken over.

Tsvangirai immediately responded by accusing Mugabe of threatening commercial agriculture in the country. 'The people of Zimbabwe are the ones [who] are going to be short-changed by an irrational leader, an irrational government,' he commented.[24]

He also criticised South Africa's ruling ANC for their claim that the level of pre-election violence was exaggerated, and for their endorsement of Mugabe's land policy. Referring to a newspaper article authored by the ANC's secretary-general Kgalema Motlanthe, Tsvangirai said: 'The ANC's endorsement of Zanu-PF is counter-productive. We would have hoped they would have done all in their power to back a free and fair election.'[25]

When the voters' roll was finally made available for inspection, it became clear that thousands of young black and white Zimbabweans – who in the main were MDC supporters – had been disenfranchised. Without any consultation they had been left off the voters' roll. As voters checked their names against the voters' roll, they found many irregularities. Hundreds of people who had died since 1994 were still on the roll.[26] In other cases, people found themselves left off the roll even though they had registered. Sometimes their names had been admitted to a supplementary roll that would only permit them to vote in the presidential elections of 2002. However, in a rare concession, Mugabe told a rally just prior to the election that those on the supplementary roll would be able to vote. Tobaiwa Mudede, the Registrar General, said that there were 5,1 million people registered for the election.[27] This was undoubtedly based on an inflated voters' roll.

The Mugabe government continued to make it as difficult as possible for the election to be properly monitored. The accreditation of foreign observers was an integral part of this process, yet they were only allowed to apply for accreditation twelve days before the election.[28] Until they received this accreditation, the observers were not permitted to begin work. In addition, for the first time since independence, foreign observers and international media representatives were required to pay a registration fee of US$100.

Even when this fee was paid, not all observers and commentators were granted accreditation. The Zimbabwean government refused to accredit the Washington-based National Democratic Institute, the World Council of Churches, the International Catholic Peace and Justice Commission and many NGOs. It also declined to accept observers from Britain, as well as Kenya and Nigeria.[29] As the international community condemned Mugabe's election tactics, Thabo Mbeki finally spoke out. 'We want free and fair elections in Zimbabwe. We are against stolen elections,' he said.[30]

Just prior to the June poll, and with hundreds of foreign observers present, the MDC was forced to cancel political rallies because of the interference of government supporters. It was impossible for the MDC to campaign in up to 50 of the 120 constituencies. Tsvangirai had personal experience of the obstacles facing MDC workers when he visited Murehwa. He described his experience:

Yesterday I was in Murehwa ... the area is totally
besieged. There were some 3 000 war veterans in the area
terrorising the populace. When we moved into Murehwa,
the police moved in ahead of us, there were thousands of
people sitting, standing and huddling in the corridors of
that community too terrified to come forward ...

I say to the people of Zimbabwe that we will win this war through the ballot box. The weapon you carry is the pen with which you make your cross. We will overcome this terror. The people of Zimbabwe carry the power to make a change. I believe in their courage.[31]

In the ten days before the election, intimidation reached new heights. Tsvangirai told the media:

We have information that Zanu-PF is going to target 30 constituencies to burn and destroy documents, to burn people's homes and to generally attempt to intimidate voters ahead of the election. We don't believe these strategies will deter all people from voting. However, the burning of identity documents makes it impossible for people to vote.

And too, we have President Mugabe saying that he will nationalise mines. He has no constitutional right to seize anything – by making these statements he is creating irreparable harm to the country. Who wants to invest in a country where property rights are uncertain? He has threatened farm property, he is now threatening the mines – where will it end? Is he nationalising the entire economy?[32]

Typical of the intimidation practised on farm workers were instructions from war veterans who said that farmers must provide their workers with transport and that they would be under the direction of a 'commander' who would take them to the door of the polling station – thus intimating that their vote would not be secret.

A week prior to the parliamentary polls, Tsvangirai addressed a capacity crowd of 45 000 people at Rufaro Stadium in Harare. In a watershed speech, firmly establishing him as representative of Africa's 'new guard', Tsvangirai said:

> ... There is a new wind whispering through the people of Africa. We suffered under colonialists but after nearly 50 years of uhuru across Africa, we find terrible oppression has come from the African leaders who were supposed to liberate us. The people of Africa are saying – No More – we want our freedom NOW ...
>
> Now is the time to rejoice because of the courage of ordinary people. I have travelled the length and breadth of this country. I have seen women who have been raped by Hunzvi's war veterans, I have spoken with people whose houses have been burnt, I have seen farm workers being force-marched into re-education camps, having been beaten and traumatised to support Zanu-PF. I have seen proud men beaten in the streets like dogs and what I have seen in their eyes is COURAGE.[33]

Despite the odds stacked against the MDC, the party felt that it was making some headway. The MDC had seen a massive mobilisation of volunteers of all races, and the party's efforts received widespread acclaim from the international community, which applauded the MDC's quest to restore Zimbabwe to a workable democracy.

From early morning on 24 June, Zimbabweans came out in force to vote. Tsvangirai went to cast his ballot with his wife, Susan, in his home constituency. His parents, Lydia and Dzingirai, voted at a school close to where they lived.

Shortly before voting, Tsvangirai reflected: 'The die is cast. This is the day we move forward as a country, or backward into an economic abyss. Hope is our future. We have had liberation for 20 years, but this vote is about real freedom.'[34]

Immediately as elections began there were accounts of intimidation and irregularities from around the country. These reports ranged from war veterans barricading polling stations to harassing, attacking or abducting polling agents. Some polling stations were issued with the wrong voters' rolls; in other cases, the voters' rolls were missing altogether. Some voters were told to return the next day.

As the results started to filter through, Tsvangirai and his supporters were pleased at how many seats the MDC had managed to win despite the intimidation and other electoral problems. In the end, the MDC won 57 seats to Zanu-PF's 62 seats. This was not sufficient to form a new government for Zimbabwe, but the seats won were more than the required third to block any changes that Mugabe might attempt to the country's laws and constitution.

Tsvangirai had chosen to stand in his home area of Buhera. He lost the seat by 2 534 votes, despite enormous support. The MDC later claimed that there were electoral irregularities in this constituency and took the matter to court. Eventually the result was overturned, but the ruling party then appealed and the case was referred to the High Court for a final hearing. In addition, there were more than 30 other constituencies in which the MDC contested the outcome of the elections. A series of court challenges began. Eight of these were won by the MDC but the ruling party then challenged them in turn.

Immediately after the parliamentary poll, Tsvangirai announced that he would like to see Mugabe impeached for initiating pre-election violence, which saw the death of at least 30 people. 'It was unconstitutional and a violation of the rule of law,' he said.[35]

It is no exaggeration to say that this election, in a small southern African country, gripped the imagination of people all over the world. Nobody put it better than a friend writing from Hong Kong:

A huge blow but what a magnificent showing by the MDC! In the face of insuperable odds – so much has been won. The fact that Morgan Tsvangirai stood in his home constituency – and apparently, not a safe seat – is the measure of the man. Unutterably brave and steadfast. Without electoral rigging and massive intimidation, can you imagine the result? Would be interesting to see how the seats in parliament would fall if along the lines of proportional representation – I suspect Zanu-PF might just be eclipsed.

Just. But so much achieved. It will change Zim – nothing will ever be quite the same again. And those candidates who have been so upfront and unbelievably strong, and who have now lost – my heart aches and weeps for them. And all their supporters. Please let it all come in for them some day. So many fine and decent, honourable people. The sight of those millions queuing patiently to make a difference ripped me to the core. Let their faith be vindicated, with justice someday soon.[36]

Zanu-PF's reaction to the election's outcome was to step up its intimidation of the MDC. In early September the MDC building was rocked by a grenade attack. The following week Tsvangirai's office at MDC headquarters was ransacked, and vital computer disks and documents were removed. The party immediately appealed to the High Court, which ruled the seizures unlawful, and its equipment was returned. Key MDC personnel including Nelson Chamisa, the head of the party's youth wing, and Gandi Mudzingwa, Tsvangirai's personal assistant, were arrested.

Another form of censure by the Zanu-PF government was its refusal to pay the MDC its allowance as the official opposition. In terms of the Political Parties Act, an annual allowance of Z$49 million was supposed to be paid, but this was not forthcoming. The situation was only eventually rectified about a year after the parliamentary elections.

Despite everything faced by the MDC and its supporters Tsvangirai remained upbeat. On his return from a successful lobbying trip in Europe, Tsvangirai said: 'The mood [in Zimbabwe] is tense. We are caught between a restless population and an arrogant government'. President Mugabe 'has been resilient so far but for the first time he is facing the real possibility of losing power'.[37]

Tsvangirai's European trip was key in eliciting support for the opposition. The message from those whom he met with in Britain, Scandinavia and Ireland was clear: these countries would not support Zimbabwe until Mugabe stood down.

Tsvangirai's assertion that Mugabe was losing power was strongly backed by a poll conducted in November 2000 by the Helen Suzman Foundation. It indicated that Zanu-PF's support, particularly in rural areas, had fallen dramatically.[38] Mugabe gave no indication that he was worried about this loss of support. He officially voiced his hatred of whites and their 'black puppets' in the MDC at the Zanu-PF Congress in mid-December. 'Our party must continue to strike fear in the hearts of the white man, our real enemy. Down with the whites,' he roared in Shona.[39]

Violence continued at endemic levels in the country. Up to the end of July 2001, some 19 000 people had been adversely affected by the continuing conflict. Mobs of Zanu-PF supporters, armed with pickaxe handles, barbed-wire whips and AK-47 rifles, had caused chaos with only rare interventions by police.[40] The Zimbabwe Human Rights NGO Forum claimed that Zanu-PF officials and supporters were responsible for 95 per cent of the crimes while the MDC was blamed for 2 per cent.[41]

However, none of these people faced prosecution as Mugabe ordered that no legal action be taken against thousands of supporters and officials of his ruling party. An amnesty gave free pardon to every person liable for prosecution if he or she had been involved in a politically motivated crime excluding murder and rape committed up to 31 July 2000.

Someone who was not immune to prosecution was Morgan Tsvangirai. Back in September 2000, Tsvangirai had told a crowd at a rally that if Mugabe did not step down as president of Zimbabwe, should he not go peacefully, he would be removed violently from office. The state alleged that Tsvangirai was guilty of advocating terrorism. If convicted on these charges, Tsvangirai could spend the rest of his life in prison.

In May 2001, the Zimbabwean High Court referred the case to the Supreme Court, accepting Tsvangirai's position that freedom of speech – a constitutional matter – was at stake.[42]

The next challenge that Tsvangirai faced was to have the Supreme Court drop the charges of incitement to terrorism, sabotage and violence. The law under which he had been charged was an anachronism. It had not been applied in more than twenty years. Ironically, it had been enacted in the 1960s to assist Ian Smith's government to suppress black nationalists including Robert Mugabe.

Tsvangirai's lawyer argued that this law now violated guarantees of freedom of expression provided for in Zimbabwe's constitution.[43] Eventually, in November 2001, the Supreme Court ruled in Tsvangirai's favour. This judgment caused much relief and jubilation in MDC circles, and added to the woes of the increasingly undermined Zanu-PF. The stage was now set for a Tsvangirai–Mugabe show-down in the upcoming presidential elections.

4

The Presidential Election

Prior to the March 2002 presidential election, the MDC's final Bulawayo rally was held at White City in Bulawayo's western suburbs. The area was packed with 10 000 people, most wearing white MDC T-shirts, sitting on the ground and in the stands. Morgan Tsvangirai sat with the MDC executive. He seemed in an upbeat mood and appeared confident of victory.

The rally was a peaceful and orderly affair. Right in the middle of Tsvangirai's speech which began grandly with 'We are now crossing over the River Jordan ...', an army helicopter flew over the field and circled around several times, causing the crowd to jump to their feet chanting 'Chinja Maitiro, Izenzo Gukula – Chinja' ('Change the way you do things. Change your behaviour. Change'). They gave the aircraft the open-handed MDC salute. Clearly the crowd thought that Robert Mugabe was in the helicopter on his way to the nearby Barbourfields Stadium where Zanu-PF was holding its final Bulawayo rally before the election.

Over at Barbourfields people waited for Mugabe to arrive. Loughty Dube, the Bulawayo Bureau chief for the *Zimbabwe Independent*, spoke to a ZBC cameraman, who said that he had been sitting at Barbourfields all afternoon and they were still waiting. Apparently people were being forcibly bused in from various parts of Bulawayo's suburbs as well as from the outlying areas.

This was a coercive tactic employed by Zanu-PF throughout the pre-election period. People were loaded onto buses by sheer force or by threatening them and their families with starvation – and then taken to Zanu-PF's rallies or political education meetings up to 150 kilometres away. In many instances the deal did not include a return journey, and people would be expected to find their own way home.

The following day, in Harare, 50 000 people willingly attended the MDC rally while less than 10 000 attended the Zanu-PF rally in the city. The message was clear: Bulawayo and Harare appeared to be unequivocal MDC strongholds.

In addition, polls predicted a landslide victory for the MDC,[1] and the party's field-workers reported a huge shift towards the MDC in most of the accessible areas. In particular, the tide was turning in Tsvangirai's favour in Masvingo province. This contained Zimbabwe's largest rural population, and the results of the presidential election likely rested on this region.

Faced with such strong opposition, Mugabe and Zanu-PF resorted to three principal tactics in the run-up to the election. In the first place, they continued to deploy war veterans and youth militia to stir things up and to intimidate people in traditional MDC strongholds as well as in areas faithful to Zanu-PF such as Mashonaland East.

The closer the election loomed, the more the MDC executive, MPs, party workers and supporters were tested. They were continually harassed by the Zanu-PF militia, as well as by the 'war veterans', some of whom were too young to have seen conflict in the bush war. From October 2001, when it was clear that the presidential election would definitely take place, until February

2002, 56 deaths were attributed to political violence.[2] In addition, there were reports of rape, torture, kidnapping, property damage or theft, cases of intimidation, schools being forced to close, as well as accounts of deaths or executions.

While the independent press often exposed these reports, the state media effectively ignored, and failed to publicise, them. Investigations by the Zimbabwe Human Rights Forum revealed that the forces primarily responsible for the widespread violence were the war veterans and youth militia. More worrying to the MDC executive was the fact that the Zimbabwe police were often found to be party to these acts of violence against MDC workers and supporters.

In early February, while distributing leaflets in Nkayi for Morgan Tsvangirai, three MDC MPs, Abednico Bhebhe, MP for Nkayi, Peter Nyoni, MP for Victoria Falls, and Joel Gabuza, MP for Binga, were abducted, beaten and tortured for two days. They were then arrested by the police and paraded – injured, bleeding and wearing handcuffs – in front of the Nkayi police station. At the same time, 37 party officials and supporters were also arrested.

Abednico Bhebhe was seriously injured. This was the second time that he had been attacked in this way. Just prior to the June 2000 elections, he was abducted and beaten unconscious. Although several bystanders witnessed this incident, no arrests were made. When he returned to Nkayi the following year to campaign for Morgan Tsvangirai in the presidential election, he arranged to go in a large convoy for protection.

In spite of Bhebhe's efforts, and possibly because of the support that he garnered for the MDC, Nkayi became a hotbed of intimidation. Bhebhe related one tragic story of how a couple, who ironically happened to be Zanu-PF supporters, had been severely beaten, simply because the Zanu-PF militia assumed that they supported the MDC. The wife had decorated the exterior walls of their home with a pattern of handprints. The open hand is the symbol and salute of the MDC, signifying the movement's commitment to non-aggression.

Zanu-PF's plan was to recruit some 200 youths in each of the 120 constituencies – nearly 25 000 young people. The MDC's information manager, Nkanyiso Maqeda, told a reporter from the London *Independent* newspaper that Zanu-PF was recruiting core groups for training in gun handling and shooting, as well as delivering political lessons in patriotism and history. Central to their training were military tactics and political indoctrination. All recruits were offered a chance to join the army in exchange for assisting with Robert Mugabe's re-election campaign.

Immediately prior to the election, Burnside – a previously peaceful Bulawayo suburb – became the temporary home of hundreds of Zanu-PF militia. They camped *en masse* in the open, in close proximity to people's houses. This caused a great deal of alarm among the residents, who were unnerved by the singing of militant Zanu-PF songs at all night 'pungwes' – indoctrination meetings that were often rounded off with protracted wolf-like howling, a traditional Shona terror tactic that could be heard kilometres away. But Burnside was not unique: this happened in many other urban areas.

In the run-up to the election, the key to keeping safe, especially if you lived in rural areas of Zimbabwe, was to have a Zanu-PF card. Then costing Z$100 each, they were, and still are, the best insurance a person can have against harassment and grievous bodily harm. On some white-owned farms, the entire workforce became Zanu-PF members, sponsored and joined by the farmers themselves.

Workers had their lives and work disrupted by the compulsory attendance of political re-education pungwes in order that they might not be evicted from their jobs and their farms. When travellers were stopped and searched, if they did not have a Zanu-PF membership card, they could have their identity cards confiscated – one of the Mugabe government's ploys to prevent MDC supporters from voting. Villages and townships were raided too and confiscations of identity cards occurred.

This was part of the second tactic that Mugabe employed prior to the presidential election: to frustrate and disenfranchise as many voters as possible. The government knew that the higher the poll, the more likely it was that the vote would swing to Tsvangirai.

Consequently, at the start of 2002, thousands of Zimbabweans already registered on the voters' roll were summarily disenfranchised. In July 2001 the Citizenship Amendment Act was passed. Under this Act, many Zimbabwean citizens were forced to renounce their right to the citizenship of a foreign country in order to retain their Zimbabwean citizenship. Some would-be voters had been born overseas but had lived in Zimbabwe for decades. Others had been born in Zimbabwe but were entitled to, though had not claimed, citizenship of a foreign country.

People were given until 6 January 2002 to renounce their foreign citizenship fully or lose their Zimbabwean nationality. Although this move by the Registrar General, Tobaiwa Mudede, was mainly aimed at disenfranchising Zimbabwe's white population, who were seen by the government as potential MDC voters, it also had the same effect on countless black Zimbabweans who had been born outside the country. Remember that tens of thousands of black Zimbabweans lived in exile during the years of the bush war, and many had children while they were living outside

the country. Also affected were the many thousands of professional black Zimbabweans who were living in economic exile in countries around the world.

All of these groups, targeted by the government for disenfran-
chisement, had been entitled to participate in the June 2000 general election – with a large percentage of them actually able to
exercise their vote.

The confusion of the Citizenship Amendment Act, and the
lack of information disseminated outside Zimbabwe's main centres, resulted in as many as one million people being unable to
vote in the presidential election. Even if they were aware of the
new restrictions, many people did not have the resources to
ensure that they were not struck off the voters' roll.

In an attempt to halt this development, Morgan Tsvangirai
took the Registrar General, Tobaiwa Mudede, to the High Court
at the end of December 2001. Tsvangirai argued that it was not
necessary for people with a claim to foreign citizenship to have to
renounce it.

Mudede insisted that he was entitled to require such people to
renounce their foreign citizenship or be removed from the voters'
roll. But the judge ruled that the citizenship amendment legislation did not apply to a Zimbabwean citizen with claim or entitle-
ment to foreign citizenship. Tsvangirai then applied to the High
Court to have the 6 January 2002 citizenship deadline extended.
However, on 10 January, the Minister of Justice announced that
the voters' roll had been closed and that the presidential election
would take place on 9 and 10 March 2002.

At the end of January, registered letters, costing Z$80 each,
were sent by registered post to 20 000 Zimbabwean citizens who
had purportedly renounced their Zimbabwean citizenship.
Informed that their names had been removed from the voters'

Morgan Tsvangirai comforting a relative of Tichoana Chimenya, his polling agent, who was killed with a collague in the run-up to the parliamentary elections in June 2000. (Photo courtesy of Topper Whitehead.)

Morgan with his wife and his brother Samuel on his wedding day in July 1978. (Photo from family album.)

The Tsvangirai family at home in Harare. Standing: Edwin Rumbidzai, Vambai, Garikai; seated: Susan, the twins Vincent and Millicent and Morgan. (Photo courtesy of Topper Whitehead.)

Morgan and Susan Tsvangirai ploughing the fields at the family homestead.
(Photo from family album.)

Tsvangirai speaks at an MDC rally at Hwedza in the run-up to the parliamentary elections in 2000. (Photo courtesy of Topper Whitehead.)

David Coltart, human rights lawyer and MDC MP, and his wife Jenny at the funeral of murdered farmer Martin Olds. (Photo courtesy of Topper Whitehead.)

Morgan Tsvangirai, MDC vice-president Gibson Sibanda, and party chairman Isaac Matongo at the launch rally of the MDC in 1999.

An MDC gathering prior to the 2005 parliamentary elections. (Photo courtesy of William Bango.)

Susan Tsvangirai, standing in front of an MDC election poster of her husband at a rally prior to the 2000 parliamenatary elections. (Picture: Topper Whitehead.)

Morgan Tsvangirai addressing a rally in Harare in 2000.

MDC supporters at a Harare rally in March 2005. (Photo courtesy of William Bango.)

Morgan Tsvangirai speaks to the crowd in front of the coffin of his slain polling agent, Tichoana Chimenya. (Photo courtesy of Topper Whitehead.)

roll, they had seven days to appeal against this removal to the constituency registrar.

This exercise cost the cash-strapped Zimbabwe government Z$4 million. Even more problematic was the fact that rural blacks were not sent these letters at all. Their names were removed from the roll without their being notified of the fact. Many people arrived at the polls with valid Zimbabwean ID cards, showing them to be bona fide Zimbabwean citizens, only to be refused permission to cast their votes.

The MDC was not prepared to accept matters as they were. In the three months prior to the election, Morgan Tsvangirai and his legal team spent much of their time in the High Court challenging government rulings.

On Thursday 7 March, two days before the election, 3 000 hopeful Zimbabweans, desperate to be able to cast their votes, brought an urgent application in the High Court in Bulawayo. Most of these applicants, but not all, were white. In the end, a ruling by High Court Judge Chiweshe was passed down on Friday night that stated that all Zimbabwean citizens should be allowed to vote, a right that they were not always able to exercise in practice.

In addition to deploying war veterans and disenfranchising voters, Mugabe resorted to a third tactic in the run-up to the presidential election: he worked to discredit and harass his principal opponent. Propaganda campaigns were stepped up in urban areas, widely seen as MDC strongholds. Much of the government's propaganda against the MDC stuck. Although people might vote for Tsvangirai, some referred to him jokingly as Tsvangison – the derogatory name given to him by Mugabe and by pro-government publications implying that Tsvangirai was Tony Blair's 'tea boy' or lackey.

Tsvangirai also experienced increasing harassment as the election drew closer. In December 2001, the CIO raided his home at 3:00 a.m. They climbed over a wall into his property and pulled everyone out of bed, searching the house for any incriminating evidence. They left empty-handed, somehow overlooking Tsvangirai's briefcase that had been put down next to his armchair when he came in the night before.

Mugabe was desperate for something with which to damn Tsvangirai in the upcoming election. If he could not unearth any genuine evidence, his next gambit was to manufacture some.

A month or so before the election, reports began to circulate that Tsvangirai had been charged with treason for plotting to kill Mugabe. At this point, he had not actually been charged; the rumours that abounded were part of Zanu-PF's campaign to dissuade people from voting for Tsvangirai as the new president.

Campaigning was also made extremely difficult for Tsvangirai. Just over a week before the presidential poll, he held a rally in Chiredzi, after which he started doing walkabouts in the various settlements between Chiredzi and Masvingo. The first two stops went off without incident, but by the time he got to the third, the police appeared.

'They started hurling teargas at us and we had to get into our cars and leave. They were shooting in the air and then proceeded to chase us for about 250 kilometres, virtually the whole way to Masvingo,' he recalled.

'On another occasion, we were campaigning in the Kadoma area, and a whole lot of Zanu-PF youths started throwing rocks at us. One large rock broke the side window – in fact, I caught it in my hands! How you are supposed to legitimately canvas for an election, I just don't know.'

As the pre-election campaigns drew to a close, there were other disquieting indications of things to come. At Bindura, before voting had even begun, a police van was involved in an accident. The doors of the vehicle burst open and thousands of ballot papers – all already marked – fell out. Comparable stories filtered through from elsewhere in the country, but polling stations nevertheless opened on the morning of Saturday 9 March 2002.

Voting in the Bulawayo area was fairly peaceful despite the truckloads of Zanu-PF youth militia moving between the polling stations – some attempting to vote more than once and, in some instances, actually managing to cast a vote although their names were not recorded on the voters' roll.

Throughout the weekend in the Bulawayo area, many reports were received of electoral irregularities, but by the time reporters got to the scene, the alleged perpetrators were usually long gone. In one incident, the e-tv television reporter Kalay Maistry was alerted to the fact that a group of Zanu-PF women in Bulawayo's western suburbs were offering to pay people to vote Zanu-PF. Maistry was taken to a house in Mpopoma where a group of women sat around a table covered in lists of names and ID numbers. They denied any wrongdoing, but a woman was interviewed who confirmed that she had been offered money to vote for Robert Mugabe.

Despite the many problems, the co-operation between opposition MPs and ordinary citizens from all walks of life was extraordinarily courageous and heart-warming. Many Zimbabweans volunteered their help, their vehicles and their cellphones to ensure that mobile polling stations would be closely monitored.

Farmers from the rural areas assisted in areas where they were unknown to the local population. This was done to avoid possible post-election retribution. In places where farmers helped out in their home district, this retribution at times became a reality. One tragic example of this was the murder of Norton farmer Terry Ford. The image of him lying dead, with his Jack Russell curled up alongside, was captured on film and broadcast to the world. Shortly after Ford's death, his farm was handed to Robert Mugabe's sister Sabina.

Masvingo was always considered the province that could make or break the election. The lack of access in rural areas to the independent press in part explains why Zimbabwe's rural population has been slower to reject Zanu-PF as a viable government. Only state-controlled newspapers, such as *The Herald* and *The Chronicle*, are freely distributed in Zimbabwe's rural areas and they have only disseminated government propaganda since before the June 2000 election.

On the second day of voting, Graham Nish, involved in running the MDC Masvingo province command centre, predicted an MDC landslide in Masvingo. Voters, previously very cagey about their political affiliations, were coming out of the voting booth and flashing the MDC salute. These people had been too frightened to openly declare their support for Tsvangirai, but now they began to sense safety in numbers. Nish commented that they were effectively coming out of the political closet.

In Harare, in particular in the densely populated suburb of Chitungwiza, there were scenes of voters who were peacefully waiting for the polls to open, being teargassed by police. The turnout in these areas was particularly high, but the voting process was unnecessarily slow, with only 2 000 to 3 500 voters being able to cast their votes at many polling stations over three days. Despite the Electoral Act's requirement to allow all voters present at the close of polls to cast their vote, tens of thousands were summarily disenfranchised when the stations were closed. Some people had been waiting for up to twenty hours to vote.[3]

Even given gross inefficiency, it was not unreasonable to expect a higher volume of voters to have been processed, leading the MDC and many observers to claim publicly that it was the deliberate aim of government to allow as few people as possible to vote. As part of this aim, the number of voting stations in Harare was reduced, and Tsvangirai has subsequently said that he believes 'that up to half the people trying to vote in Harare were not able to cast their vote'.

As the second day of voting, and Tsvangirai's fiftieth birthday, edged to a close it was clear that thousands of people would be unable to vote. Tsvangirai was again in the High Court, this time to appeal for an extension of time. Before ruling in the MDC's favour, the judge insisted on taking a helicopter trip to see the state of the queues in the Chitungwiza area. Even when voting was allowed to carry over into a third day, many election officials did not immediately obey the order and some not at all. On Monday 11 March, some polling stations chose only to open at noon. Voters had been queuing since the early hours of the morn- ing – not to mention the previous two days.

As voters gathered to cast their ballots, Tsvangirai toured the polling stations to lend his support. The frustration was tangible as he heard their complaints about having queued since 4:00 a.m., and being barely closer to voting some twelve hours later.

Thousands of Zimbabweans working in South Africa made repeated trips home, firstly to register on the roll and then finally to cast their vote, though many found themselves thwarted from doing so in one way or another.

Outside Harare, although voting was fairly orderly, there were widespread incidents of intimidation, alongside the harassment of polling agents and domestic observers.

Morgan Tsvangirai was worried by the direction in which

events seemed to be heading. He met with Sam Motsuenyane, who headed the South African Observer Mission. 'At that point, I thought that even if the election turned out to be rigged, the South Africans would denounce it as such,' reflected Tsvangirai in June 2004. On the night of 11 March 2002, he issued a public statement in which he commented:

> I thank you for your courage as you continue to vote in your millions. We see your determination. We hear your support. We share your impatience. The power is in your hands. What the people of Zimbabwe now deserve is a celebration ...
>
> But the forces of darkness may yet try to block your path to victory.
>
> As I address you, it is sad that this regime still seems intent on defying your will. Whatever may happen, I as your loyal servant am with you all the way. They may want to arrest me and at worst kill me, but they will never destroy the spirit of the people to reclaim their power ...
>
> The tide of change is irreversible but we must be prepared to pay a high price for our freedom. President Mugabe and his colleagues are afraid of the people and we have heard they may do anything to kill the messenger. If they do, you must stay strong and carry on the work we began together. Among you walk heroes – heroes who waited hours and hours to vote, heroes who refused to be turned away. These are the heroes of the new Zimbabwe whose voices must be heard around the world.
>
> Now is the time we have been waiting for and we are ready. But let us first wait peacefully for your votes to be

cast and counted. Restrain yourselves so you do not allow
their sinister plans to succeed. As you wait for the results,
do not succumb to their provocative traps. I know they
are trying very hard to provoke you. Yes, we share your
fear that the result will be rigged, but let us complete the
process we began together in our campaign for a better
life for all Zimbabweans ...

The Meikles hotel in Harare was the nerve-centre of the foreign press corps, and many people waited there for the announce-
ment of the poll results. Counting started on Tuesday 12 March,
and at this point many were still hopeful of an MDC victory.
However, after the weekend's events and the widespread reports of
poll rigging, Morgan Tsvangirai feared the worst.

That night there was live coverage as the election results came
in from counting stations all around the country. The first results
from Umzingwane, in Matabeleland, were Mugabe 5 883,
Tsvangirai 11 226. Reports of dozens of similar victories in urban
seats then started to come in. MDC supporters' elation was, however, to be short-lived. The results that came in thereafter from the
remote rural areas were overwhelmingly in favour of Zanu-PF. In
addition, some of the results initially announced were later
changed to reflect wins for Zanu-PF.

As the broadcast progressed, people were shocked to find individual results being altered as they went along. Although this was
an indication of poll rigging, the general opinion is that the principal doctoring was crafted prior to vote counting. There is consensus that the actual counting process was done in an orderly
fashion, monitored by the various observer missions. However,
the stuffing of the many boxes that were not attended at all times
by all parties is pretty much a certainty. Bill Johnson, a political

commentator and the former director of the Helen Suzman Foundation, said in his report on the election:

> But most of all there was ballot stuffing. As one examines the results, one can see that this must have gone on quite generally. In the MDC strongholds of Harare, Bulawayo and the two Matabeleland provinces not only was turnout down but, in the last two months when 400 000 names were clandestinely added to the rolls, the numbers registered in these four provinces either stagnated or actually fell – an astonishing outcome ... Given that the officials in charge of the polling stations were ... all handpicked for their government loyalties, the insertion of these boxes would not have been difficult. Then in nine of the 120 counting stations, the MDC agents watching the account were jailed, assaulted or driven away. In all nine cases there were large and unaccountable increases in the turnout – with over 60 000 extra votes cast than the doubtless already inflated totals for 2000 [parliamentary election] – massively in favour of Mugabe.[4]

On Wednesday 13 March the MDC held a press conference in the Meikles hotel at 11:30 a.m. The conference room was packed with the foreign press corps – a battery of television cameras was set up in front of the table where the MDC would sit. The atmosphere was predictably electric.

By now it was apparent that the MDC had lost, and that the elections had probably been rigged. Poignant scenes accompanied the raw reality of defeat. For security reasons and to avoid the crush of the press, Tsvangirai entered the Meikles hotel through the back entrance, slipping into the conference room via the kitchens. The Meikles' kitchen staff were excited to see him. With hope etched on their faces, they greeted him with the open-handed salute of the MDC, amidst a chorus of 'Chinja, Chinja'. Tsvangirai looked at them and wordlessly shook his head.

When he entered the conference room, he looked absolutely exhausted and admitted that he felt 'awful'. He told the assembled gathering that he had planned to be giving his victory speech. Instead, he accused the presidential poll of being the 'biggest electoral fraud in history'. The MDC was unequivocally rejecting the result. Tsvangirai commented:

> The MDC is firmly of the view that the election results for the Zimbabwe presidential election, as announced by the Registrar General's office, do not reflect the true will of the people of Zimbabwe and are consequently illegitimate in the eyes of the people. We therefore do not accept them.

When asked by the media whether he was planning to leave the country in light of the impending treason charges, he reiterated:

> We are not going any where – we will not abandon our people – we remain firmly committed to a democratic and peaceful path, which we will pursue to the end ... Together we will complete the change for a better life for all Zimbabweans. The power is in our hands.

In most elections, even in Zimbabwe, the law provides for public inspection of the voters' roll. It took the Zimbabwe Civic Education Trust (Zimcet) four court orders to enable public access to a copy of the roll. Another three court orders, obliging Mudede to make available a copy of the supplementary voters' roll, were ignored. The MDC applied to the Supreme Court for the supplementary roll to be discounted, but Chief Justice Godfrey Chidyausiku, picked by Mugabe to replace Chief Justice Anthony Gubbay, declined to make a ruling on the matter.

The voters' roll eventually made available to Zimcet had a total of 5,2 million voters. This register was supposed to have been closed at the end of January, but in the two months prior to the election, Zanu-PF managed illegally to register an additional 400 000 voters in the rural areas. This brought the final roll to around 5,6 million voters, a total that has to be viewed as highly suspicious.

A 1997 census illustrated that Zimbabwe had 12 million inhabitants. If we take into account that over 60 per cent of Zimbabwe's population are under 16, that large numbers of adults live abroad in economic exile, as well as the crushing impact of Aids, the conclusion is that there are probably less than five million Zimbabweans of voting age. A local market research company established that a maximum of 80 per cent of adults are registered to vote at any given time.[5] If we accept all of these variables, it seems as though at least 1,8 million registered voters on Mudede's voters' roll cannot exist. It is these fictional voters who appear to have tilted the vote in Mugabe's favour.[6]

Zimcet decided to conduct an audit of the voters' roll. This revealed that only 50 per cent of the names on the roll actually lived at the given addresses – an essential requirement to vote in any particular constituency.

If we accept Zimcet's assessment of half the voters no longer being resident and consequently being disenfranchised, there should have been no more than 2,5 million eligible voters in the 2002 presidential poll. Given that a maximum of 80 per cent would actually cast their votes, the maximum number of voters should have totalled around two million. Yet, according to Mudede, more than three million people actually voted with 1 688 939 voting for Mugabe; 1 254 930 voting for Tsvangirai; and the other three hopefuls garnering 31 179, 12 367 and 12 169 votes respectively. In addition, there were nearly 50 000 spoilt papers.[7]

This evidence suggests that the million or so manufactured votes would have favoured Mugabe. It is not likely that Tsvangirai would have won any less than the number of votes announced. Based on these projections, it seems that the more realistic result would reflect 700 000 votes in favour of Mugabe, and 1,3 million votes cast in favour of Tsvangirai.

A vital contributor to Zanu-PF's success in derailing a free and fair poll was the fact that the MDC's polling agents were denied access to many polling stations. To compound matters, the Zimbabwe Electoral Support Network, headed by Reginald Matchaba-Hove, and with more than 12 000 trained monitors on hand, was told a few days before the election that these monitors would be denied involvement in the polling process. Instead, the government appointed 450 untrained and inexperienced monitors, some drawn from the ranks of the Zanu-PF youth militia, to watch over 4 500 polling stations. The MDC polling agents had to keep 100 metres away from the polling stations, which rendered effective observation impossible. In addition, the majority of election officials in charge of polling stations 'were army, police, civil servants or war vets selected for their pro-government loyalties'.[8] Complicating matters further was the decision in Harare to combine the presidential election with municipal elections. The government had kept delaying the Harare mayoral elections, fearing that they would follow the lead of Bulawayo, Masvingo and Chegutu where the MDC enjoyed huge victories.

If the same were to happen in Harare prior to the presidential election, the result might influence the outcome.

So many international journalists covering the 2002 presidential election, as well as members from various foreign observer missions, witnessed incidents and evidence of gross intimidation, alongside massive polling irregularities. Zanu-PF youth militia attacked two members of the South African Observer Mission who were meeting MDC representatives in KweKwe. Shortly after this, a minibus carrying SADC Parliamentary Forum observers was stoned by Zanu-PF youths outside Chinhoyi where they had attended an MDC rally. Three observers were injured.

Yet even with first-hand experience of intimidation and violence, the South African mission, led by Dr Sam Motsuenyane, announced at a press conference on 13 March that they considered the whole electoral process to have been legitimate. The night before, so Tsvangirai recalls, Motsuenyane had come to him to say he had completed his assessment, confirming that the results of the election reflected the will of the people. He asked Tsvangirai to sign the report. 'I was flabbergasted. I said to him, "Why should I sign the report?"'

When Motsuenyane made his pronouncement at a press conference, it was greeted with stunned silence followed by laughter and shock at what the journalists had heard. Motsuenyane did not comment on the free and fair – or otherwise – nature of the election. He simply took pains to stress that the South African Observer Mission recognised the election's legitimacy.

A week later, during the South African parliamentary debate that was shown on television, various members of the Mission took to the podium to relate their experiences in Zimbabwe. A few expressed their anger at the interim verdict of Motsuenyane's team. One of those voicing disapproval was the fiery and respected Patricia de Lille, who castigated certain members of the team for not doing their job. She said that on more than one occasion she had spotted them sitting in the foyer of the Zanu-PF stronghold, the Harare Sheraton. Returning some hours later, she found them still sitting in exactly the same spot.

The day after the results were announced, the mood in Zimbabwe was sombre. It was not uncommon to find people in tears. The thought of having to endure Mugabe for another six years was just too much.

People hoped that at least the violence would stop. Instead, the youth militia stepped up their campaign, punishing those who had supported MDC during the election. Three MDC workers, including a polling agent, 27-year-old structural engineer Zenny Dube, were abducted and buried alive in a bush pit. Another MDC polling agent, 32-year-old James Nevana, was abducted the day the voting ended and was taken to a Zanu-PF militia camp. His death brought to ten the number of MDC polling agents murdered in March 2002.[9]

Despite everything, when I visited Morgan Tsvangirai at his Harare home, he was as ebullient as ever and in a positive mood. It was pointless lying down like a beaten dog, he said. It was time to plan ahead and to keep fighting. Although mindful of the lingering treason allegations, he stressed that he would not leave the country or his people: 'We are in this together and we must carry on.'

Trudy Stevenson arrived. She is Zimbabwe's only white female MP, hugely respected by her constituents, and admired for her bravery. She walked into the room and greeted Tsvangirai as 'Mr President'.

She articulated what so many people knew to be true: Morgan Tsvangirai should have been the legally elected president of Zimbabwe.

5

The Aftermath

Zanu-PF supporters celebrated as Mugabe was sworn in as the president of Zimbabwe for another six-year term of office. However, those Zimbabweans who had cast their votes in a different direction were dismayed by the election's results. People waited, many with little hope, to see how the situation in the country would unfold.

The ripples caused by the election and its outcome were not confined to Zimbabwe. In the broader African and international arena debate around events in the country and its future was fierce. Shortly after the election, Mugabe and Tsvangirai were approached by President Thabo Mbeki of South Africa and President Olusegun Obasanjo of Nigeria. They hoped to persuade the two men to agree to a compromise, in a bid to avert Zimbabwe's suspension from the Commonwealth.

Obasanjo commented: 'Whatever Zimbabweans have done, whether they have voted or not, they need to eat. They need international assistance and that help will not come unless the leaders put their arms together to work for the country.'[1] Tsvangirai responded that a government of national unity would only have validity if it represented a transitional period, paving the way for free and fair elections. 'It is time for the nation to heal, but there is no way it can be healed without democracy,' he remarked.[2]

Then the Commonwealth Observer Mission released a hard-hitting report on the presidential elections.[3] It declared that Zimbabweans had not been able to vote freely because of state-sponsored violence, a partisan police force and repressive legislation. Prior to the election it had been agreed that if this mission were to report adversely on the election, the Nigerian, South African and Australian leaders would be authorised to suspend Zimbabwe from the Commonwealth.

Accordingly, on 19 March 2002, the Commonwealth suspended Zimbabwe and called for new elections. The decision was taken in view of the manipulation of the presidential elections and human rights' violations.[4] Obasanjo acknowledged that there had not been 'adequate provisions' in the elections to allow everyone to express their will.[5]

After much deliberation with the MDC's executive, Tsvangirai agreed to the appeal from Mbeki and Obasanjo to hold talks with Zanu-PF. On a personal level, he was not keen on dialogue; an attitude shared by many of the younger, more militant-minded MDC supporters. The MDC made it clear that it was only interested in talks if they would lead to a transitional government, with a mandate to hold new elections under the watchful eye of the UN or the Commonwealth.

Before any negotiations could be finalised, on 20 March, Tsvangirai was arrested on charges of treason. He was taken to Harare Central Police Station, fingerprinted and charged and released on bail of Z$1,5 million. The case (discussed in Chapter 6) would take nearly a year to come to trial.

Hopeful of paving the way for big Western investment in the African continent, yet with the crisis in Zimbabwe ever persistent, a summit of fifteen African leaders met in Abuja, Nigeria, towards the end of March to endorse a declaration on democracy and good governance. The draft document was to commit African leaders to ensuring a free press, an independent judiciary, and a dedicated and efficient civil service. A strong commitment was pledged to eradicate corruption and to respect human rights.[6]

With US$64 billion needed for the New Partnership for Africa's Development (Nepad), described as 'The Marshall Plan of Africa', Thabo Mbeki, as one of its key architects, recognised the need for African governments to adhere strictly to the principles of democracy. However, Zimbabwe represented an embarrassing problem and, being unable to get Mugabe to toe the line, Mbeki must have known that his vision for Nepad could be threatened. Accordingly, leaders attending the one-day summit in Abuja agreed to set up a new body to enforce standards for governance in Africa. Unfortunately, the new body did not have any impact on the way that Robert Mugabe governed his country.

When Nepad was eventually presented at a G-8 summit in Kananaskis, Canada, in June 2002, it met with reservations. Had the Zimbabwe crisis been resolved satisfactorily, the reception might have been a lot warmer. In the end, Mbeki had to fight to sell his vision. Instead of walking away from the summit with US$64 billion for Africa, G-8 leaders committed themselves to a mere US$6 billion, deliverable by 2006. Central to the West's lukewarm reception of Nepad was Africa's record in dealing with Zimbabwe. In a letter to the *New York Times* on 1 July 2002, Ed Royce, Chairperson of the Subcommittee on Africa in the US State Department, said:

[T]he response to the Zimbabwean crisis is undermining the [Nepad] programme. Zimbabwe is on the precipice of a devastating famine of Robert Mugabe's making, the latest of the illegitimately re-elected president's ploys to maintain power. African leaders, with a few exceptions, have been silent. Until they show a commitment to the programme's goals, Zimbabweans and other Africans will pay the price.

Ordinary Zimbabweans certainly were paying a price on several fronts. People were faced with increasing repression and levels of violence as well as a failing economy in which inflation and food shortages spiralled rapidly out of control. Four weeks after the election, many Zimbabweans took to the streets to protest against the election's outcome and to demand a new constitution and fresh presidential elections. The demonstrations, collectively organised by the NCA, the coalition of trade unions, professional organisations, student bodies and church groups formed in 1998, gathered in cities and towns around the country.

In a typical response, Mugabe described the protests as senseless and Home Affairs Minister John Nkomo issued an edict banning them. More than 400 people, including women and children, were arrested as they met to plan the demonstrations.

Those who had supported the MDC also found themselves the target of violence and intimidation by the Zanu-PF youth militia and so-called war veterans. As an example, the human rights NGO, the Amani Trust, reported that about 1 200 polling agents, registered as monitors for the MDC, were unable to remain in their homes. Whole communities were literally on the run.[7]

Another measure of repression directed against MDC supporters involved the politicisation of food aid distribution. Zanu-PF supporters hijacked the distribution of maize from the Grain Marketing Board, diverting the grain trucks to the homesteads of those chiefs and village headmen who were perceived to be loyal to the ruling party.[8] This resulted in thousands of people being starved merely because they came from families who did not support the ruling party. In particular, children who were meant to benefit from supplementary feeding schemes found themselves targeted. Sam Mlilo, the district chairperson of Mberengwa East, was quoted as saying: 'Children with parents sympathetic to the MDC are denied access to food. In each village there are some MDC supporters, and the villagers ... drive their children away'.[9]

The food shortages were not, however, confined to MDC supporters. Zimbabwean bankers Stanbic announced that the country needed Z$16,5 billion if it were to feed the 7,8 million people in the country who were in the throes of starvation. Stanbic further cautioned that Zimbabwe's huge domestic and foreign debt made it extremely difficult for the government to pay for various schemes, including food imports.

People faced a desperate struggle when trying to feed their families as escalating inflation rendered their money worthless, and food shortages widened across the country. It is hard to explain accurately what an average family needed to survive on. As a rough idea, in December 2002, the minimum wage for a domestic worker was Z$4 000. A small chicken, enough to feed six people if eked out, cost Z$2 000. A kilo of rice cost another Z$2 000. Loughty Dube, reporter for the *Zimbabwe Independent* in Bulawayo and chairperson of the Bulawayo branch of the Zimbabwe Union of Journalists, commented:

I am one of the more fortunate ones as, in Zimbabwean terms, I earn a good salary. Yet I cannot eat breakfast anymore – you cannot buy bread. It takes hours to queue for just one loaf and then it costs nearly $200. Milk also

costs $200. I wait until lunchtime and buy myself a plate
of *sadza*, meat and vegetables. That sets me back $600
each day. The majority of people in this country are not
getting a single meal each day.

The food crisis was accompanied by an increasingly short supply of fuel that saw people queuing for hours, even days, to keep
their vehicles on the road. Mugabe's efforts to secure a new line of
finance from Libya were in vain. Libya had previously been a
source of credit, but the country now refused assistance due in
part to Zimbabwe's inability to pay its debts, as well as Mugabe's
tarnished profile, which was rather compromising at a time when
Libya was trying to regain respectability within international
ranks.

The government did not seem to have a plan to alleviate the
food shortages. In fact, the issue of farm evictions and land invasions – disruptive to the domestic production of foodstuffs –
began to gather momentum. All farmers who had been served
with eviction notices, legally or illegally, were told to cease production and leave their farms. Many were terrorised by gangs of
war veterans and Zanu-PF thugs, mainly drawn from the youth
militia. Those still occupying their farms were told that they had
to vacate their land by 8 August 2002. The impact of these 'land
reforms' on the 250 000 farm workers, all with families and
dependants, was crushing. Most were summarily evicted. They
lost their homes and their livelihoods, often along with access to
education and healthcare.

Since the fast-track land-grab had begun in 2000, many farmers had fought to stay on their land but, for some, the battle now
became too great. They packed up and left, usually doing what
they could to provide for their employees. However, many domes-

tic and farm workers were abandoned far from their family villages and homes, with compensation often proving inadequate for relocating families and their possessions to safety.

A large proportion of farmers, disgruntled at the Commercial Farmers' Union's decision to drop all litigation against the government, formed a new organisation, Justice for Agriculture (Jag). The organisation undertook to shun any negotiations that could imply recognition of Mugabe's legitimacy. Jag also resolved to sue Zanu-PF for property losses incurred since the farm invasions began.

One Karoi farmer, Andrew Kockett, appealed in the High Court to have his eviction order overturned. Judge Charles Hungwe ruled the eviction order invalid, saying that the government had failed to serve the eviction notice on Kockett's bank to which the farm was mortgaged. With at least 90 per cent of farmers mortgaged to financial institutions, the ruling effectively annulled most of the eviction orders that had been served.[10]

In the days following the August deadline, which affected 2 900 farmers, hundreds were arrested and imprisoned for not vacating their farms by the due date.

In the midst of the escalating domestic crises, Tsvangirai and the MDC executive were busy working on a programme aimed at strengthening the party. For some time the MDC had been on the receiving end of criticism that, in the post-election period, they had not been 'doing anything'.

Tsvangirai admitted that with the arrest and subsequent death in prison of Learnmore Jongwe, the MDC's press adviser, he and the MDC had been remiss in communicating effectively with the public. He also found himself hampered from visiting certain areas of the country due to his bail restrictions arising from the treason charges, which required him to report to the police in

Harare every second day. Similarly, international travel was not possible, as his passport had been confiscated. However, much-needed work was being done to consolidate and strengthen the party from within, giving its MPs increasing support so that they, in turn, might support their constituencies more effectively in the face of ongoing persecution and famine.

January 2003 dawned with a renewed sense of vigour and purpose on the part of the MDC executive. In mid-January Tsvangirai confirmed that government representatives had approached him back in December, proposing talks on power-sharing.[11] At the time he had roundly denounced the plan, but he now agreed to entertain the idea. In December 2002, he recalled:

The process really is three-pronged. One is that we – the Movement for Democratic Change and Zanu-PF – agree that Mugabe has become such a liability that the nation cannot move forward, so he has to retire. Secondly, it means that, in terms of the constitution, within three months we must go to elections. In the end, we all know that conditions are not ideal for conducting a free and fair election, so we need some time so that the [right] conditions are created, the constitution is amended and that normal political activity stops lawlessness and returns the country to some national confidence.

The last part is that, at the end of all this, we must have free and fair elections, which will then give the people of Zimbabwe an opportunity to elect their own government.

In response, Mugabe was quoted as saying that it would be counter-revolutionary and foolhardy for him to step down just months after a fiercely contested election. He further stressed that exile was not an option for him.[12]

As political tensions continued to grow, an unexpected twist came in the form of the World Cup Cricket tournament. Hosted by the South African Cricket Board in early 2003, some of the games were scheduled for play in Harare and Bulawayo.

Henry Olonga, the Zimbabwean right-arm fast bowler, and his team-mate Andy Flower, decided to use the occasion to protest against the rapid deterioration in their country's economy and human rights status. Accordingly, when they took to the field for the Zimbabwe–Namibia match in Harare, they registered their discontent by wearing black armbands, indicating that they were in mourning for the death of democracy in their 'beloved Zimbabwe'.

After his protest, Olonga was banned from playing any further games in Zimbabwe and he was forced to become a political refugee from his own country. The Zimbabwe Cricket Union also tried to bar Flower from playing any further matches, but three of his white team-mates rallied round him and said that if Flower did not play, they would not do so either.

Once the World Cup furore had faded somewhat, the MDC concentrated on pressing forward with mass action. There were those who asked why the MDC had not shut down the country in the immediate aftermath of the abortive presidential election. The answer was simple: persuaded that dialogue was crucial, the MDC was sincerely committed to breaking the deadlock with the ruling party. Until this proved futile (which it did when Zanu-PF called off the talks initiated by presidents Mbeki and Obasanjo), the MDC was determined to keep the lines of communication open.

The first stayaway was held in March and was highly effective, with an estimated 80 per cent of the country's industrial and commercial operations closing down for at least two days. The *Daily News* reported: 'Business was brought to a virtual standstill in the major cities as the nation heeded the opposition MDC's call for a protest to press President Mugabe and his government to confront the worsening economic situation and stop the violence against dissenting voices.'[13]

The government backlash was not long in coming. Gibson Sibanda, vice-president of the MDC, was arrested for the part he had played in arranging the action. It took some time for his bail to be granted. At Khami prison he was kept in solitary confinement as it was feared that he would be a 'bad' influence on his fellow inmates.

Eventually Sibanda was released on bail. There to support him at his court hearing were Morgan Tsvangirai and Paul Themba Nyathi, a member of the MDC executive and spokesperson for the party. No sooner had the successful bail hearing been heard than the police arrested Nyathi as he left the court. He was held in the cells at Bulawayo Police Station and only released some days later when a magistrate ordered that there were no grounds for his arrest and detention.

In a concurrent instance of governmental crackdown on the opposition, the MDC MP for Kadoma, Austin Mpandawana, was held in the police cells at Kadoma for weeks on end. He was arrested during the first stayaway of 2003 and, like Sibanda, he faced charges relating to the Public Order and Security Act. He was denied bail when charged and his appeal against being held in custody was referred to the High Court. His legal counsel was then informed that his case was not urgent – meaning that he could wait indefinitely for his case to be heard. He was finally released in August and died shortly thereafter, apparently from injuries sustained while in custody.[14]

Tsvangirai described this stayaway as the 'Zimbabwean people's Rubicon'. With the party now ready to 'finish the job', he confirmed that the MDC had never been in better shape. It was now preparing for what Tsvangirai optimistically called the 'final push'.

Much thought and discussion went into the planning of the next round of mass action. The beginning of June 2003 was finally decided on. It was felt to be financially much easier for people to risk not being paid at the start of the month, with a full month's salary behind them. As it was, many employers allowed their staff to stay away on full pay.

The week-long mass action was thwarted by a massive clampdown by the government. In Harare, a crowd of around 5 000 people gathered to march from Highfields towards the city, but they were dispersed by police who were heavily armed with weapons and teargas. At the University of Zimbabwe, thousands of students tried to demonstrate, but they were also prevented by the police, who used teargas to disperse the crowd.

Bulawayo saw more of the same, as did other centres around the country. While the state-owned media dismissed the mass action as a failure, the police and military forces were out in unprecedented and heavily armed numbers. Contemptuous though the media might be, the government was leaving nothing to chance.

Indeed, a legal wrangle had been fought out in the courts as to the legality or otherwise of the protests. The Commissioner of Police applied to the High Court for an order to declare the planned protests illegal. The High Court issued an order banning the protests on the evening of Saturday 31 May 2003. However, early on the Monday morning, with the mass action scheduled to begin, the MDC filed an appeal against the High Court's order.

The appeal was accepted. Under Zimbabwean law, once an appeal has been filed against an order, and accepted, the order becomes null and void. As such, in a legal context, the protests were entirely legal.

Zanu-PF, realising its folly, went back to the High Court on the Thursday evening, the penultimate day of the mass action, and successfully persuaded the High Court to issue another order that cancelled the right of appeal against the previous order. This ultimately rendered the protests illegal but could not be applied retrospectively.

As MDC spokesperson Paul Themba Nyathi pointed out:

Not only are assertions that the MDC defied court orders dangerously misleading, so too are reports that the ultimate aim of the week of mass action was the forced removal of the Mugabe regime. This was not our aim. The MDC cannot impose a new government or leader on Zimbabwe. Only the people themselves can do this through a free and fair election. The aim of the mass action was to peacefully bring pressure to bear on Mugabe and his regime to enter into unconditional dialogue aimed at resolving the crisis of governance in Zimbabwe. Mass action is a process and we will continue to engage in all forms of peaceful civil disobedience until meaningful dialogue commences.

The most significant outcome of the mass action was the arrest of Tsvangirai, on a *second* set of treason charges (the trial for the first set of charges – described in Chapter 6 – was running at this time) for his involvement in the mass action and for allegedly encouraging the overthrow of the government.

He spent more than two weeks in prison in the middle of winter – only permitted to wear a shirt and shorts. In fact, he had arrived at Harare Central Prison wearing a fleecy tracksuit top, but was immediately made to take it off. When he protested that many of the other prisoners were wearing the same kind of top, they too were forced to remove their warm clothing.

Tsvangirai was crammed into a cell with 75 other inmates. At night there was barely room for them all to lie down. The latrine in the corner was always overflowing and the thin blankets they were given stank of urine and were infested with lice.

Despite these hardships, Tsvangirai describes this time as an amazing life experience for him. He took the opportunity to talk to the group collectively, laughingly calling these sessions 'rallies'. Like so many political prisoners before him, he was imprisoned with criminal prisoners. Many of these men had been inside for a long time. Many stayed inside because they had nobody to pay their bail demands.

On a piece of toilet paper, Tsvangirai wrote down the names of the men affected in this way as well as their bail requirements. When he was released, he handed over the list and money from his personal accounts to his lawyer, Innocent Chagonda, asking him to bail the men out and to organise them legal representation.

Eventually, he was released on bail on this second set of treason charges. In order to have him released, the MDC had to pay bail of Z$10 million in cash. In addition, it had to provide Z$100 million in guarantees. This meant that the party reluctantly had to put up the title deeds of its Harare headquarters, Harvest House, as surety.

When the news of these stringent bail conditions got out, the party was inundated with offers from ordinary Zimbabweans, some offering Z$1 000, while other donations were as much as Z$500 000. The response was heartening. As MDC secretary-general Welshman Ncube said at the time: 'This is reassuring to us as to where people stand. They are willing to cushion us from the attempt by the state to bankrupt us.'[15]

Just prior to Tsvangirai's release, the South African government, in the face of pressure from the West, approached Harare about the possibility of having him released. It also broached the subject of the resumption of dialogue between the two parties. For some time, the MDC had been earnestly preparing to resume talks with the ruling party.

When, a few weeks after Tsvangirai's release, President Mbeki announced at a joint press conference with US President George Bush that the MDC and Zanu-PF were 'talking' to each other, an MDC press statement was issued repudiating this claim. The statement said that since the aborted talks back in April 2002, there had been absolutely no political engagement between the two political parties.

The South African and international media were taken aback. Investigation revealed that the statement had apparently been erroneously sent out by a zealous worker in the MDC information department. The communiqué had not been cleared by William Bango, who was also in Johannesburg at the time.

In fact, President Mbeki was quite right as an ongoing, informal programme of shuttle diplomacy between the two parties had been taking place, although direct dialogue had not yet commenced. Paul Themba Nyathi explained that this engagement between the two parties had been facilitated by the South African High Commissioner in Zimbabwe, Jerry Ndou, as well as by church groups and NGOs.

At the time of President Bush's visit to South Africa in June

2003, the entire executive of the MDC, except for Welshman Ncube and Morgan Tsvangirai (the former's passport was in police hands and the latter was in prison), were in Johannesburg for meetings with members of the US State Department. Contrary to rumours being spread by Zanu-PF supporters that there were succession disputes within the top ranks of the opposition, the MDC delegation was unanimously behind Tsvangirai as president of the MDC.

All in all, the South African trip was a success for the MDC. It emerged that there was a meeting of minds between presidents Bush and Mbeki regarding, firstly, the urgency of the Zimbabwean crisis and, secondly, the requirements to resolve the crisis. The MDC delegation returned to Zimbabwe with renewed hope and encouragement.

In the meantime, the day-to-day activities of the MDC continued and the focus moved to the upcoming council and mayoral elections that were to be held on 30 and 31 August 2003. In these polls, despite reports of voter intimidation and a low voter turnout of 30 per cent, the MDC virtually swept the board, gaining control of all the major urban centres, except KweKwe and Kadoma.

David Coltart, the MDC MP for Bulawayo South, described the results as follows:

On the Friday, Zimbabwe's ruling party, Zanu-PF, controlled every single municipality in the country, except for Harare. On Tuesday, the reality was that the MDC now controls the municipalities of Harare, Bulawayo, Gweru, Masvingo, Victoria Falls, Kariba (which now has a white mayor, John Houghton), Gwanda, Ruwa and Hwange. In Chegutu, where there

is an MDC mayor, power is shared with Zanu-PF as
every single MDC candidate was prevented from filing
his registration papers. [This was also the case in Bindura
and Rusape.]

Coltart continued:

The MDC now controls the budgets and operations of
Zimbabwe's five largest cities, its two major tourist resorts
and several other strategically important towns. Roughly
40 per cent of the country's population live in these
centres that generate 50 per cent of the country's GDP.
    Whilst the MDC won parliamentary seats in all these
cities and towns in 2000, that never translated into
control – because MDC MPs have always been in a
minority in parliament and were powerless to prevent
the ruling party from passing laws and budgets to their
liking. For the first time, the MDC has gained total
control over the areas it first won largely symbolically
in 2000.[16]

The government-appointed electoral registrar in Bulawayo,
Willard Siyenda, was praised for his fairness when it came to
counting disputed votes. Lack of voter education had caused a
large number of ballot papers to be incorrectly marked. Ticks
instead of crosses, with some of them not exactly in the box, were
noted. In almost all cases Siyenda saw the intention of the voter,
mostly in favour of the MDC, and allowed them to be counted.
    When the time came to announce that the MDC had won in
all of Bulawayo's 29 constituencies, Siyenda stood on the steps of
the City Hall and did his duty. When he had finished, the large

crowd started singing and dancing with joy as the contingent of army and police personnel looked stolidly on.

As Coltart summed up the results of the election: 'The desire of Zimbabweans for liberty is a tidal wave that cannot be stopped. The events this past weekend will soon swamp this brutal regime and force it to yield. Freedom is now just around the corner.'[17]

Unfortunately, just two weeks after this MDC victory, on 12 September 2003, hopes for democracy and the right of free speech were dealt a blow when Zimbabwe's only independent daily newspaper, the *Daily News*, was closed down by the government. This newspaper had started publishing in 1999 and had become synonymous with the fight for democratic and press freedoms. In 2000 and 2001, the paper's offices were attacked with bombs, the second attack destroying its printing presses.

The *Daily News* was told that it could not continue operating unless it applied for registration, under the draconian Access to Information and Protection of Privacy Act, to a commission whose members were appointed by Jonathan Moyo. Up to that point, the daily newspaper had been published without this licence in defiance of the March 2002 law. The *Daily News* had already appealed to the Zimbabwe Supreme Court against registration because it deemed some sections of the Act to be unconstitutional.

After its closure, the *Daily News* applied for a licence, which was rejected by the Media Commission. The courts then ruled that the newspaper should be licensed by the end of November, and could continue publishing in the interim. On 25 October the newspaper was back on sale again, but was shut down again shortly thereafter and the case went back to the courts.

The closure of the *Daily News* came right after the renewal of the debate on the country's eligibility for readmittance to the

Commonwealth. This had occurred in the light of the MDC's victories in the council and mayoral elections, as well as assurances by South Africa's President Thabo Mbeki that Mugabe would strive for political and economic reform as well as an improvement in the country's human rights record. The closure of the *Daily News* was most definitely not a step in the right direction and, in December 2003, the nations involved voted that Zimbabwe should remain suspended from the Commonwealth.

This verdict – indicating that there had been no substantial improvement in Zimbabwe's international standing – was a telling confirmation of the fact that in the 21 months that had passed since the presidential elections, the country had been racked by ongoing domestic crises that showed no real signs of abating. Now the world waited for the outcome of Tsvangirai's treason trial.

6

Is this Treason?

The treason charges laid against Tsvangirai on 20 March 2002 were based on a series of supposedly treasonable meetings that had taken place between Tsvangirai and one Ari Ben-Menashe, of the Montreal-based firm Dickens & Madson, between September and December 2001.

These meetings were first brought to the public's attention in a television exposé made by journalist Mark Davis for Dateline, a current affairs programme on Australia's SBS channel. The exposé was aired on 13 February 2002.[1] Davis, 'a journalist honoured for his work in East Timor and other difficult spots',[2] claimed to have watertight proof that Tsvangirai, in a meeting with political lobbyists Dickens & Madson had plotted to kill Mugabe. Footage was shown of alleged discussions to eliminate Mugabe. Certain words were not audible or were wiped out completely. All reference to Mugabe's elimination was mostly made by the use of subtitles. The sound was poor although you could hear Tsvangirai use the word 'elimination' once or twice. Davis also claimed to have audio proof of an assassination plot, saying that he had audiotapes of two meetings held between Ben-Menashe and Tsvangirai in London.

Tsvangirai issued a statement on 14 February in which he said:

The MDC [was] approached by Dickens & Madson who said they wanted to help build the MDC's image abroad, but mainly in North America, where Mugabe was said to be winning the propaganda war through his lobbyist group, Cohen & Woods, which according to Dickens & Madson, was paid the sum of US$5 million for the purpose of repairing Zanu-PF's tattered image.

Rupert Johnson, a contact of Renson Gasela, the MDC's Shadow Minister for Agriculture, had introduced Dickens & Madson to the MDC. The two men had known one another when Gasela was the general manager of the Grain Marketing Board, and Johnson was operating as a South African-based commercial trader.

A total of three meetings were held with Dickens & Madson, two in London and one in Montreal. At the first meeting, Ari Ben-Menashe said that the group wanted to help the MDC on the communications front. He also told Tsvangirai that he had previously been hired by the Clinton administration to negotiate an exit deal for Robert Mugabe. Mugabe had initially accepted the package but had later reneged before the parliamentary elections in June 2000.

In his press statement of 14 February Tsvangirai went on to say: 'At no stage, during the first three meetings, was the issue of elimination or assassination ever discussed.' He continued that Dickens & Madson do not dispute the fact that he'd burst out of the room when he became disturbed at the approach they were taking in the meeting. He did not know for sure, but suspected that hidden cameras were recording the meeting.

After the third meeting Tsvangirai briefed his colleagues about the lobbyists' suspicious conduct. This resulted in a belated back-

ground check on the firm and on Ben-Menashe. It was then dis-
covered that Ben-Menashe had written a book called *Profits of
War*, on dirty political tricks, and that he had been hired by Zanu-
PF to 'set up' the MDC under the guise of potential MDC
lobbyists.[3] When these facts became known, the MDC cut off all
communication with Dickens & Madson in December 2001.
The party maintained its commitment to peaceful and constitutional change of government.

Aside from this official version of events, there was far more to
the situation, as Tsvangirai revealed in discussions in July 2002.

According to Tsvangirai, it all began in August 2001 when
Renson Gasela was contacted by Rupert Johnson. Gasela suggested: 'Since we are going to run a presidential campaign, we may
need some help. Some people have approached me who may fit the
bill. May I take this further with the secretary-general [Welshman
Ncube]?' Tsvangirai gave him permission and then the conversation was all but forgotten. At the end of September, Welshman
Ncube and Morgan Tsvangirai agreed to meet Rupert Johnson at
the Hilton Hotel at London Heathrow's Terminal 4. This was the
first time that the pair had met Johnson and Ari Ben-Menashe.

Recalled Tsvangirai:

Ben-Menashe's first point of introduction was his involvement with Clinton in ensuring that Mugabe exited
the political scene gracefully. He also said that he was
desperately disappointed when Mugabe eventually
refused to stand down and retire.

He seemed so thoroughly on the side of the MDC
and its democratic principles. He came armed with a
survey conducted by the *Financial Gazette* saying he
understood that Zimbabwe desired a change in govern-

ment and was sympathetic to the MDC's cause. He also said the MDC seemed in a strong position to win the election but wanted to know how the MDC was going to deal with the military and how was I going to deal with Perence Shiri, the commander of the air force and former cadre of the infamous Fifth Brigade.

The understanding was that Ben-Menashe would negotiate with the Zimbabwean military to ensure their full support in the event of my winning the presidential election in 2002.

At this point, Ben-Menashe said that in order for his firm to start work for the MDC, a contract would have to be signed with a deposit of US$100 000 paid over. The full fee would be US$500 000.

We said we'd have to make some calls. Welshman and I left the room to phone Zimbabwe. We discussed the matter with our treasurer, Fletcher Dulini-Ncube, and we all agreed that we did need help in promoting the MDC in North America, to counteract the adverse information that was being disseminated there on behalf of Zanu-PF. We came back into the meeting and signed the contract. Rupert Johnson signed the contract on behalf of Ari Ben-Menashe.

A second meeting took place in October when Tsvangirai flew to London 'literally for the day' to meet with Johnson and Ben-Menashe. He explained:

The reason I made such a concerted effort to get there was that I was told of a new development they wanted to discuss with me ...

I was, however, stunned when they told me that, because of the events after 11 September in the United States, they had not been able to get a meeting with Colin Powell. I was irritated that they could not have sent me a fax or telephoned me with this non-information. We had just scraped the barrel to pay the US$100 000 deposit for their services, and now I was wondering whether we had made a mistake. Something did not feel right.

In early December 2001, Tsvangirai travelled to Montreal to attend a third meeting with Dickens & Madson. Originally he was told that the meeting would be in Washington so he could meet influential people in the US State Department and thus lobby support for the MDC. Tsvangirai described events:

The idea was we were to meet the next day at 11 a.m. at Dickens & Madson's offices. When Ben-Menashe and Johnson came to collect me for the meeting, my intuition told me something was not right. I can't think whether it was something in their demeanour that made me uneasy but from the moment they collected me, I felt that something was amiss.

Arriving at the firm, I was ushered into the board-room. There were six of us in that meeting: Ben-Menashe, Rupert Johnson, Alexandre Legault, Tara Thomas, Ben-Menashe's assistant, Ben-Menashe's partner at Dickens & Madson and a gentleman who was introduced to me as 'Mr Simms, a senior director of the CIA [Central Intelligence Agency], with responsibilities for Africa'. This also made me feel uneasy as it was totally unexpected.

Tsvangirai jumped right in and opened the meeting by saying, 'Now where are we?' Ben-Menashe replied by asking, 'Have you met with the military yet?'

'Again, I was astonished,' Tsvangirai said in July 2002. 'This was supposed to be his job, something we had paid him precious forex [foreign exchange] to do. However, I cautiously told him that we had some contact with military personnel, but nothing on an official basis. At that point, Ari blew up at us and started shouting irrationally.'

According to the official transcript, later prepared from the audiotape of the meeting for Tsvangirai's trial defence team in 2003, Ben-Menashe said: 'Look, sorry, we are not hired guns neither are they [meaning Simms and Johnson] going to murder Mugabe and then assassinate or eliminate, or whatever, and then come back and say now there is a constitutional process. This isn't what we do for a living, to assassinate the head of state.'

Tsvangirai replied to Ben-Menashe: 'I am certainly agreeing there. The arrangement really is, when we last met at the RAC club, we agreed that the route we were going to take was that if Mugabe goes, there will be a transitional arrangement, but the method of implementation was not discussed.'

Ben-Menashe then asked: 'Who do you think on the ground is going to approve a transitional arrangement?'

Tsvangirai said: 'Well, it was not clear, it was not precise.'

Ben-Menashe countered: '... Work has been done on your behalf in Africa up to Congress, work has been done to get these guys on side for the elimination on your behalf and over, but what about ... all the work that has been done, the inside work?'

At this point Tsvangirai could see what Ben-Menashe was getting at and got up and walked out of the room.

'Rupert Johnson ran after me and begged me to come back. I

suspected that the meeting was somehow being recorded. At that point I should have left the building. But Ben-Menashe came out and said to me that Mr Simms was going to leave and if I wanted American government support for the MDC, I must come back inside. I reluctantly agreed to do so,' Tsvangirai recalled.

'The conversation resumed and Ben-Menashe introduced a new subject: Suppose Mugabe was eliminated? I replied to the effect that if something happened to Mugabe – if he dropped dead (from natural causes) – then the vice-president would take office. In terms of the Constitution, this would have to be followed within six months by free and fair elections, which, I felt, we would definitely win. All references to the elimination of Robert Mugabe were introduced by Ben-Menashe.' Again Tsvangirai was alarmed and upset. He felt Ben-Menashe was introducing issues that had nothing to do with the objectives of the company's engagement as communication lobbyists.

Rupert Johnson also brought up the subject discussed previously in London, that of getting the defence force to support a transitional arrangement should elections result in Tsvangirai winning the presidential election. As perhaps the most influential person in the defence force, Perence Shiri was earmarked as a target for negotiations to this end. Tsvangirai then said he was concerned that it would not be possible to broker an agreement between the various parties including Shiri. The conversation continued along these lines, with Ben-Menashe using the word 'elimination' at least fifteen times in the meeting.

'Then Simms said the American government was prepared to donate US$1 million to the MDC, to be followed by another amount of US$1,5 million towards the presidential campaign. Simms also asked who funded the MDC – that is outside of the subsidy it receives from the Zimbabwe government as the official opposition. He asked for our trust's account number so the money could be deposited. I phoned our lawyer in London to get the number of the trust account and then gave it to Simms. After this, the meeting broke up and Simms left.'

That night, Alexandre Legault took Tsvangirai to dinner. It was a social occasion until they were joined by Ben-Menashe, who did not order dinner, but continually pressurised Tsvangirai to pay them the balance of the contract, amounting to US$400 000. Tsvangirai refused to confirm that the balance would be paid. As far as he was concerned, nothing had been achieved so far. Until the US$1 million initially promised was deposited in the MDC's trust account by the US State Department and he had discussed the matter with the MDC executive, he would not agree to pay anything. The next day Ben-Menashe took Tsvangirai to the airport to catch his flight. He did not mention the matter of the money again. That was the last time Tsvangirai saw Ben-Menashe until the trial.

It took from 20 March 2002, when Tsvangirai was first charged with treason, until February 2003 for the case to open in Harare's High Court. During these eleven months Tsvangirai appeared in court on three occasions and the case was remanded to a later date each time. The reason for the delay was that the docket, including the alleged evidence in the case, had not been sent to the Attorney General, presumably because of a lack of evidence.

On the first day of the trial, the Zimbabwe police were on high alert as the proceedings opened amidst violent and chaotic scenes. *The Guardian*'s Andrew Meldrum said that police wielding batons had prevented diplomats, lawyers and MPs, not to mention journalists, from entering the High Court buildings.[4] Even the US ambassador, Joseph Sullivan, was initially denied entry, although he was eventually permitted to enter the court. Two journalists were arrested and various European Union diplomats were manhandled and denied entry to the proceedings.

Tsvangirai's arrival was heralded by cheers of encouragement from supporters. The police permitted him to enter the court, but barred the way of his two co-accused, Renson Gasela and Welshman Ncube, until it was pointed out that the trial could not proceed without them.

Once the accused were assembled, Judge Paddington Garwe entered, the court was called to order, and the trial began.

Leading the prosecution was the Deputy Attorney General, Bharat Patel. In his opening statement he said that Tsvangirai and his colleagues' 'opposition and desire for political power is not criminal as such but it is their desire to overthrow a government and to occupy positions through undemocratic means which is criminal. It is their unlawful desire of seeking to attain political power that the state seeks to punish.'[5]

In his opening statement for the defence, the renowned South African anti-apartheid lawyer George Bizos, pivotal in saving Nelson Mandela from the gallows in the Rivonia Trial, described the government evidence as 'heavily doctored' to implicate the three defendants. 'We agree that this is a trial with heavy political overtones and undertones,' said Bizos, outlining the defence case. 'This was a trap. The accused are innocent as they have said.'[6]

Bizos, leading the defence, was supported by two senior advocates, Chris Andersen and Eric Matinenga. The legal team was probably one of the best ever assembled in Zimbabwe. Bizos was required to register temporarily to practise law in Zimbabwe. Andersen had successfully represented three Americans arrested in 1999 on charges of sabotage and terrorism, alongside numerous other high-profile criminal matters in Zimbabwe and abroad. He also represented former President Canaan Banana, who was found guilty and jailed for homosexual assault. Matinenga had a history of successfully representing the MDC in election petitions against the ruling Zanu-PF after the 2000 parliamentary elections.[7]

There was an electric atmosphere in the courtroom on the second day as Ari Ben-Menashe took the witness stand. Beginning his testimony for the state, Ben-Menashe said that Morgan Tsvangirai had plotted a coup to depose Robert Mugabe – backed by £6 million from the British government.[8]

He told the packed court that Tsvangirai had actually asked him to assassinate Mugabe and carry out a coup, alleging that the opposition leader had told him: 'Mugabe will not leave office unless he is carried out in a coffin ... he has to be killed, it has to look like an accident and nothing to do with the MDC.'[9]

Ben-Menashe then claimed that Tsvangirai and his associates took out a US$500 000 contract for the assassination, further alleging that Tsvangirai, once president of Zimbabwe, would guarantee Ben-Menashe's firm contracts worth about £20 million.

Ben-Menashe said he had set up an operation to secretly record video evidence against Tsvangirai, the MDC secretary-general Welshman Ncube, and MP Renson Gasela. He then said it was only later that he was hired by the Zimbabwean government to improve its image. He also claimed at the time of giving evidence that the Mugabe government owed him US$365 000.[10] Declaring that Tsvangirai had confirmed the British government would foot a £6 million payment to the Zimbabwe air force commander, Perence Shiri, to lead a coup against Mugabe, Ben-Menashe confessed he did not know what had happened to this money.[11]

In his second day on the stand Ben-Menashe implicated the American government in the intrigue. Hinting at US involvement in the alleged plot to kill Mugabe, Ben-Menashe said that a senior official from the CIA, Edward Simms, had attended the meeting in Montreal. At the meeting Ben-Menashe had introduced him to Tsvangirai as the deputy-director for Africa. (This status was never confirmed by the CIA.)

The court was then shown a grainy, barely audible black and white videotape of the alleged proceedings in Montreal. On the first day of screening, only the first half-hour was watched as the tape was repeatedly rewound to listen again to parts that were hard to hear.[12]

The pace hotted up on the trial's fourth day as George Bizos began his cross-examination of Ben-Menashe.

The day before, testifying for the prosecution, Ben-Menashe had claimed the MDC agreed to a ten-day timetable to kill Mugabe with the assistance of the CIA. With reference to this claim, Bizos accused Ben-Menashe of being a 'fraudster' and of spinning 'untruths'. This was not the first time that such accusations had been levelled at the Israeli. As a result of various activities in the previous ten years Ben-Menashe had been referred to as, amongst other things, a 'notorious chronic liar',[13] and 'an abject liar'.[14]

Bizos told Ben-Menashe that his reputation for dishonesty and fraudulent behaviour had actually put his credibility on trial. He said: 'There is a similarity between the fraud we say was committed against the MDC and its office bearers, and other frauds committed by the witness and his companies, by interfering in high-profile political matters, getting money, and then turning the tables against the people to whom the fraudulent representation were made.'[15]

During Bizos's cross-examination, Ben-Menashe failed to answer questions on many occasions. He also offered 'I don't know' or 'I don't remember' as responses to questions posed by Bizos, and even shouted abuse at Bizos at times, requiring that Judge Garwe call him to order.

When Bizos approached the matter of Ben-Menashe's new contract with the Zimbabwe government, the latter confirmed that he had been paid US$100 000 two weeks after he had delivered the videotape to them.

For its part, the Zimbabwe government refused to release details of the deal they had made with Ben-Menashe, alleging it would be prejudicial to state security. Bharat Patel produced in court a signed certificate from the Security Minister, Nicholas Goche, saying that the contract between Dickens & Madson and the government, particularly the obligations of Dickens & Madson, should not be disclosed on security grounds.

As a compromise between government wishes and the court's need to know the truth regarding the contract between Ben-Menashe and the Zimbabwe government, Judge Garwe ordered that Ben-Menashe answer the defence's questions *in camera*, closing the court to the public. Now Ben-Menashe had to answer Bizos or face contempt of court charges.[16]

In answering Bizos, Ben-Menashe admitted that he had received US$200 000 from the Zimbabwe government after providing a secretly recorded videotape incriminating Tsvangirai in a plot to kill Mugabe. However, he denied that the money was paid to him to entrap Tsvangirai. Instead, he claimed that the money was a fee for other research work performed by his Montreal firm, including intelligence and information gathering and 'background work' for the government. 'It may have had to do with the treasonous activities of the MDC, but it had nothing to do with this case,' he commented.[17]

Bizos pointed out that all the information gathered in the 26 reports Ben-Menashe claimed to have prepared for his client could have been gleaned from media reports at the time. To this Ben-Menashe replied that he could not disclose what other work had been carried out because it was 'confidential' – a term that was proving useful as an evasionary tactic.

Next in George Bizos's relentless cross-examination came the business of the audiotape, recorded during a meeting held between Ben-Menashe and Tsvangirai at the Royal Automobile Club in Pall Mall. Also present at the meeting was an employee of Ben-Menashe, Tara Thomas, who apparently made the recording and then transcribed the tape for Ben-Menashe.

According to the *Mail & Guardian*, George Bizos described a transcript of this London tape, as 'probably the most important document in the trial'.[18]

'It negates completely evidence by this witness [Ben-Menashe] on what happened at the London meeting,' Bizos said. Nowhere in the transcript supplied to state prosecutors by Ben-Menashe was reference found to the killing of Mugabe.

Ben-Menashe said his assistant complained to him that much of the tape was inaudible. '[The assistant] gave up marking points where it was inaudible and picked up words here and there and put sentences together,' [Bizos] said, adding that 'nothing on the tape could be relied on'.[19]

By his thirteenth day on the stand, Ben-Menashe was understandably exhausted. Nobody had expected the trial to last this long, and the proceedings were only on the prosecution's first witness.

The start of the afternoon session found Ben-Menashe asking Judge Garwe to be excused on the grounds of exhaustion and ill-health. He made this appeal after the judge had said he would rule on whether or not Ben-Menashe might be released from the trial, to 'attend to urgent family business in Montreal'.

Finally, more than three weeks after the start of the trial, Ben-Menashe admitted to the court that he had set out to entrap Morgan Tsvangirai.[20]

Under cross-examination, Ben-Menashe said he and his colleagues had pretended to be ready to help assassinate President Robert Mugabe ahead of the presidential election of March 2002.[21] Ben-Menashe also admitted he could not recall Morgan Tsvangirai using the words 'murder', 'assassinate' or *coup d'état* during the secretly filmed December meeting in Montreal. In fact, he suggested that it did not matter whether Tsvangirai had used those particular words. In addition, he also said that he 'could not remember' whether or not Tsvangirai had directly asked for his assistance in the assassination of Robert Mugabe. Nonetheless, he contended that it remained clear to anyone watching the inaudible videotape that Tsvangirai and his colleagues (not present at the Montreal meeting) wanted his, Ben-Menashe's, help in eliminating President Mugabe.[22]

Bizos was quick to point out that nowhere in the videotape, or in the state transcript of it, was there any evidence that Tsvangirai had asked Ben-Menashe to murder or assassinate Mugabe. There was also no evidence that Tsvangirai had asked for help to plan and execute a *coup d'état*.

With this, Judge Garwe adjourned the trial for a week so that Ben-Menashe could return home to Canada.

When the trial resumed, Bizos continued his relentless cross-examination of Ben-Menashe. In particular, the defence team focused on inconsistencies within the Montreal videotape – specifically the point at which Tsvangirai left the meeting.

Ben-Menashe initially said that Tsvangirai had stormed out of the meeting when he realised that Dickens & Madson lacked the capacity to carry out the assassination. He later changed the scenario – suggesting that Tsvangirai had walked out because he felt insulted by statements that implied he was unclear about what he wanted Dickens & Madson to do for him.

At the end of March the trial was adjourned until mid-May. When it resumed, the head of the CIO, Happyton Bonyongwe, testified that Ben-Menashe had lied about the contents of the London audiotape. He said he could not hear the MDC leader utter the words 'kill', 'murder' or 'assassinate' on the tape.[23]

At this point the trial took a strange twist when Tsvangirai was re-arrested on a fresh charge of treason for his involvement in the mass action happening at the time (discussed in Chapter 5), and for allegedly encouraging the overthrow of the government. This time bail was not forthcoming for about two weeks and each day he attended court from his cell.

The eighth witness to appear for the state was the commander of the airforce, Perence Shiri. He claimed he was offered money by the MDC to pacify generals and members of the army in the event of an opposition presidential victory in 2002.

Shiri's name was mentioned on the Montreal tape, according to a transcript in which Tsvangirai asserted that his Shadow Defence Minister had met the Zimbabwean Defence Minister along with Shiri and the army chief, Constantine Chiwenga, 'to smooth the relationship and lay down our views, that the army has to remain professional'. Shiri denied that any such meeting took place, but did say he was approached by two opposition 'lawmakers' in January 2002, after they had requested a meeting with him.

In court, Shiri testified in Shona through a translator. He claimed he'd had two meetings with MDC 'lawmakers'. At the second meeting he said Tsvangirai had sent his party's secretary-general, Welshman Ncube, to explain the MDC's policies to him. He also said that one of the MDC officials present at the meeting, Job Sikhala, offered him Z$10 million to win over the country's generals and the rank and file of the armed forces to an MDC government if it won the election. He maintained that Tsvangirai wanted Shiri to be the commander of the armed forces, assuming that Tsvangirai won the poll. Shiri said he refused the offer.[24]

On the last day of the prosecution, a state witness, Edward Chinhoyi, technical and communications manager at the state-owned Zimbabwe Broadcasting Corporation, said he thought the Montreal videotape had not been tampered with. However, under cross-examination he conceded that experts in the field could digitally substitute the sound component of a videotape with different audio material.[25]

With that, after nearly five months of testimony, the trial was again adjourned. It was to be another seven months before it resumed and Tsvangirai was able to testify for the defence in an attempt to prove his innocence beyond any doubt.

This had probably been one of the most gruelling periods of his life. The mass action exercises together with the additional charges of treason and his time in prison had really debilitated him. Tsvangirai was tired, had lost a lot of weight, but was resolved that until the trial resumed, it would be business as usual for him in his role as president of the MDC.

One piece of good news (already mentioned in Chapter 5) was that, on 8 August 2003, George Bizos finally succeeded in getting the treason charges dropped against Tsvangirai's co-accused, Renson Gasela and Welshman Ncube. For a person to be convicted of treason, there have to be two credible witnesses present, and Bizos argued that this was not the case for any of the three defendants. While the court concurred in the cases of Gasela and Ncube, it insisted that Tsvangirai was not exonerated and his trial would continue.[26]

When the trial reconvened on 10 February 2004, Welshman Ncube was the first witness called to the stand. He told the court how he had first got to know Ben-Menashe. The man had introduced himself as an Israeli spy who was on a first-name basis with several world leaders, including the Iranian president and former US President Bill Clinton. Ncube was later surprised to learn that Ben-Menashe's firm, Dickens & Madson, had only recently been formed with a handful of employees and no clients. 'It was at complete variance with what Ben-Menashe had said about his connections and influence,' said Ncube.[27]

The following day, Justice Garwe admitted into evidence key documents from a legal action instituted against Ari Ben-Menashe by the MDC. In April 2003, the MDC had begun legal proceedings in Montreal to recover the money they had paid to Dickens & Madson. These documents shattered the evidence given the previous year by Ben-Menashe, who had said under oath that the assassination of Mugabe was discussed at each of the three meetings attended by both Tsvangirai and himself, on their own and with others. However, at the Canadian hearing, Ben-Menashe told the court that assassination was not discussed at the first meeting. This completely contradicted his sworn testimony to the High Court in Harare.[28]

When Tsvangirai was first charged with treason, the state had said there were audiotapes of both London meetings and a videotape of the Montreal meeting. The audiotapes were never produced in court – the prosecutors deemed them inaudible. After some pressure, the defence managed to force the Attorney General to produce transcripts of these audiotapes, full of gaps and with no evidence of assassination ever being discussed. The transcripts were found to be consistent with the claims of Tsvangirai and his two colleagues all along.

With respect to the videotape, nowhere is there any discussion of an assassination plot. The Canadian court concluded that the Montreal meeting did not stand alone evidentially. Therefore the state had to prove that the first two meetings in London had a sinister purpose. This it was unable to do.

At this point in the Zimbabwean trial, Bharat Patel announced that despite the state's best efforts, it had failed to locate Rupert Johnson, the Zimbabwe-born trader who had allegedly introduced Morgan Tsvangirai to Ari Ben-Menashe. There were no further witnesses to be called by either side.

It had been more than a year since the trial began and, finally, it was winding up. In his closing argument, George Bizos declared that the state had failed to prove any conspiracy to assassinate Robert Mugabe or to bring about a *coup d'état*. He also said that no overt act of treason had been committed, and that even if there had been a suggested 'discussion' of it, that was not enough to warrant a conviction.

Bizos repeatedly referred to Ben-Menashe as a 'liar' who was out to get money and said: 'Menashe lied from start to finish … and when this is added to his dubious background and behaviour … there can be no question that his evidence should be rejected out of hand.'[29]

The prosecution wound up its case by declaring Tsvangirai guilty of plotting to assassinate President Robert Mugabe – a crime that carries the death penalty. 'The accused committed the crime of high treason by inciting and seeking to arrange the assassination of the head of state,' said Bharat Patel, adding that the state had proved its case 'beyond reasonable doubt'.[30]

At the close of proceedings, Tsvangirai was satisfied that Judge Garwe had conducted the trial in a proper manner. The only major irregularity had been that the court's audio equipment did not function for fourteen hours of Tsvangirai's testimony and court transcripts had to be prepared from Garwe's handwritten notes.[31] If Garwe's notes were insufficient or biased, this could potentially present a problem.

With the judgment possibly more than six months off, Morgan Tsvangirai got back to his daily life. He saw to the workings of the MDC, tried to spend time with his family, and continued to report to the police three times a week, in accordance with the bail conditions of the second set of treason allegations that he faced.

As the judgment on his case drew near, he became anxious. 'Whatever the decision, it is going to be a political one,' he said in July 2004. The danger of being sent to the gallows was hard to ignore.

Epilogue

A shock awaited George Bizos, leading counsel for the defence, when he entered the courtroom with his co-counsel, advocates Chris Andersen and Eric Matinenga, to hear the judgment of Judge Paddington Garwe in the treason trial of Morgan Tsvangirai.

As usual, Tsvangirai was early and already seated in the dock. What was highly unusual was the presence of a prison warder in the dock with him. Ranged outside the dock were another four warders. It was if they were waiting to take Tsvangirai down to the cells below the court – as if they were expecting a guilty verdict.

Bizos asked Joseph Musakwa, Bharat Patel's assistant, why the warders were surrounding Tsvangirai. Musakwa shrugged his shoulders and avoided a direct reply to the question.[1]

When Bharat Patel, leader of the prosecution, entered the court, Bizos raised the matter with him. Patel told Bizos that he saw nothing improper in Tsvangirai being surrounded by warders, to which Bizos replied: 'Well, I don't think the judge will agree with you.'[2] He did not expect anything to be done about the situation, but when Patel went to call Justice Garwe he asked his junior advocate, Morgan Namadire, to tell the prison warders to remove themselves and, after a moment, they did.

Outside the court, the crowd was restless. William Bango, Tsvangirai's personal spokesperson and assistant, was one of the many people prevented from entering the building to hear the verdict. Around Bango the police were using their batons to quell the enthusiasm of the gathered MDC supporters.

Those inside the court rose to their feet as Justice Paddington Garwe ceremoniously entered the room, took his place, called the court to order with his gavel and began to deliver his lengthy judgment.

Garwe summed up the events that had brought all in the courtroom to the present moment. He recalled the first meeting in London at Heathrow airport at which Morgan Tsvangirai had come into contact with his accuser Ari-Ben Menashe. Then there was a second meeting at the Royal Automobile Club in Pall Mall, where two of the main witnesses in the trial, Ben-Menashe and his employee Tara Thomas of Dickens & Madson, had apparently made a tape-recording of Tsvangirai asking the Montreal-based political lobbyists to help him arrange the assassination of President Robert Mugabe.

Finally, there was a third meeting in Montreal where Tsvangirai met with Ben-Menashe, Thomas, Rupert Johnson, and a man named Simms who was said to represent the American government.

Then Garwe started to review the evidence and turned almost immediately to the credibility of the witnesses. With regard to the prosecution's star witness, Ari Ben-Menashe, Garwe quickly dismissed allegations made in various press articles and publications attacking Ben-Menashe's general reputation. He commented: 'All that is before the court ... are unsubstantiated allegations made in some cases by persons who are unknown. Having carefully considered the evidence, this court is of the view that the allegations suggesting a bad reputation on the part of Mr Menashe have not been proved.'[3]

Garwe went on to speak about Ben-Menashe's demeanour in

the witness box, saying: 'There is no doubt that Mr Menashe was very rude during the proceedings ... he made gratuitous remarks about the accused ... he derided defence counsel ... he remarked at one stage, that the accused has no intellectual capacity to undertake an analysis of the results of the referendum ... there were occasions [when] he appeared not to appreciate that he was in a court of law.'

The judge drew attention to the many contradictions that had emerged in Ben-Menashe's evidence, particularly with regard to the parts played by the elusive Rupert Johnson and the mysterious 'Mr Simms'. At one point he remarked: 'There are aspects of Mr Menashe's evidence that call for closer analysis.'

When evaluating the evidence of Ben-Menashe's assistant, Tara Thomas, Garwe concluded: 'Tara Thomas ... did as instructed. Neither [Menashe] nor Tara Thomas can be described as impartial. They were out to trap the accused.'

More than an hour after entering the court, the judge was eventually coming to the part that Tsvangirai had been anxiously waiting for. Garwe began to discuss what the court was required to prove.

'In respect of the first meeting, that there was a request [to assassinate Robert Mugabe or arrange a *coup d'état*]. In respect of the second, the same, but further that a sum of [US]$97 400 was forwarded "as part of the fee for the plot". In respect of the third meeting, that there were discussions in furtherance of the plot. There is no allegation that there was a conspiracy at the third meeting. The allegation is that there was a discussion in furtherance of the aforesaid plot ... the plot hatched during the first two meetings.'

Here Garwe said it was important to expand on his statement that there was no allegation of a conspiracy at the third meeting between the parties in Montreal.

At the start of the trial, the allegation in respect of this third meeting was that Tsvangirai had requested members of Dickens & Madson to arrange for the assassination of President Mugabe and to stage a military coup. Then, once Tsvangirai's co-accused (Ncube and Gasela) were acquitted because the prosecution conceded that there was no evidence of such a request, the prosecution tried to change the charge to one of conspiracy, alleging that there was an existing agreement regarding the assassination between Tsvangirai and the other people present at the third meeting. Garwe commented: 'So far as the Montreal meeting was concerned the state was not entitled at such a late hour to allege a conspiracy when all along the allegation had been one of incitement.'

At this point Tsvangirai began to feel hopeful. He leaned forward in his seat, listening intently to what the judge was saying.

Garwe then turned to the matter of whether any overt act and hostile intent on Tsvangirai's part had been proved by the state. He said the only available evidence regarding the first meeting had been that of Ben-Menashe. Where the second meeting was concerned there was additionally the evidence of Tara Thomas, but both of these pieces of testimony had to be treated with caution. Furthermore, the contract signed after the second meeting did not substantiate the claim that there had been a request to assassinate Robert Mugabe.

With regard to the third meeting which was video-recorded, Garwe went over the fact that the tape was inaudible, that there were gaps in the transcript, and that the state was relying on the testimonies of Thomas and Ben-Menashe, both of whom had been found by the court to be suspect witnesses.

'Mr Menashe in particular must have been under considerable pressure to get an admission on tape from the accused to confirm his story that there had been a request ... It goes without saying that Mr Menashe and the others who knew that the proceedings were being recorded would have steered the discussions in such a way as to induce an admission. Some of the utterances made by the accused particularly at the beginning suggest that there were statements being made that he did not agree with ... the evidence discloses a discussion but there is nothing to suggest that the discussion was "in furtherance of a previous plot".'

'Is a discussion in these circumstances treasonous?' asked Garwe. He said the state had submitted that 'even a preparatory act done with hostile intent' or 'mere signification can be sufficient'. However, he added that 'while this statement in general terms is correct, the state faces some difficulties'.

'The first and most serious difficulty is that contrary to remarks that have been thrown about during the course of this trial, the accused did not come to court to face a charge of conspiracy in respect of the third meeting. The allegation initially was that he had made the request at all three meetings. Only after the discharge of his co-accused did the state amend the charge.'

The second difficulty Garwe detailed was that at the third meeting there was no intention on the part of Ben-Menashe and the others to act on any understanding or conspiracy. Instead, they were engaged in a trapping exercise.

'The third difficulty is that the evidence does not in any event show that there was a conspiracy or a plot at either the first or second meetings ... The fourth is that a mere discussion – in furtherance of the aforesaid plot – is not, in the absence of evidence, an incitement to conspiracy, treason ... In my view, the allegation against the accused in respect of the third meeting is vague. For this reason, the state has during the trial interchangeably referred to the charge against the accused as incitement or conspiracy ...'

Garwe concluded simply: 'In the circumstances, the court must return a verdict of not guilty and the accused is accordingly discharged.'

As Judge Garwe spoke these final words, Tsvangirai stood up and left the dock. The first person he turned to and embraced was his wife, Susan. Then he approached George Bizos and thanked him as well as Andersen and Matinenga.

The relief felt by Tsvangirai was palpable. He was finally free of the treason charges that had dogged him for nearly two years and could have sent him to the gallows. He felt an enormous burden lift from his shoulders despite the fact that he still faced a second charge of treason (of which a number of his colleagues had already been acquitted) for the part he had played in arranging the mass action protests in May 2003.

When William Bango finally saw Tsvangirai emerge from the courthouse, he heaved a sigh of relief. The MDC supporters started cheering, chanting and toyi-toyiing at the sight of their leader. After Tsvangirai had made a brief statement to the media who were waiting for him, he and Susan went home. It was time, Tsvangirai said, to relax and unwind and then start planning for the future.

Postscript

The MDC entered the 2005 general elections on a very uneven playing field. Once again, essential requirements of a free and fair election were barely observed, especially in the monitoring and counting of votes. Not surprisingly, the MDC was trounced by Zanu-PF, winning only 41 seats, as opposed to the ruling party's 79.

Almost immediately the international community denounced the electoral process. Jack Straw, the UK Foreign Secretary, said it was fundamentally flawed. 'Mugabe has yet again denied ordinary Zimbabweans a free and fair opportunity to vote, further prolonging the political and economic crisis he has inflicted on their country.' Even before the Zanu-PF victory was announced, Morgan Tsvangirai said that the party did not accept that the results received so far represented the national sentiment. 'The Government has once again betrayed the people.'[1]

Losing 16 seats was a massive blow to Tsvangirai. 'I was disappointed that nothing had really changed and that the sentiment which we had gauged so strongly in the run-up to the election was being denied.' He was upset about all the constituencies lost to Zanu-PF through what he believed was electoral fraud. But one constituency close to his heart was that of Chimanimani, bravely contested by Heather Bennett, wife of imprisoned MDC MP, Roy Bennett. Bennett had been sentenced to a year in prison for pushing in parliament Zimbabwe's Minister of Justice, who taunted him about the loss of his farm. In the 2000 elections Bennett, a white farmer, had won the country's second-largest majority in this constituency.

Yet amidst the depression of electoral defeat, there was one small thing for Morgan Tsvangirai to be glad about. Two weeks after the poll and nearly five years after the gruesome murder of his polling agent in Buhera, Tichaona Chimenya, and his assistant Talent Mabika, a CIO state security agent was charged with allegedly masterminding the murder of the two.[2] Finally, justice looked as though it would be served – and that there was indeed hope for the future of Zimbabwe.

Notes

Chapter 1: The Early Years

1. Nelson, *Zimbabwe*.

2. Unless otherwise specified, all of the quotations from Morgan Tsvangirai were obtained during a series of in-person and telephonic interviews that the author conducted from 2001 to 2004.

3. http://www.giles.34sp.com/biographies/mugabe.htm

4. http://rhodesian.server101.com/Ian%20Douglas%20Smith.htm

5. *Report of the Commission on Rhodesian Opinion under the Chairmanship of the Right Honourable, the Lord Pearce.* Harare: Her Majesty's Stationery Office, May 1972.

6. Chikhuwa, *Rise to Nationhood.*

7. Moorcroft, *Thousand Years.*

8. Smith, *Great Betrayal.*

9. Chikhuwa, *Rise to Nationhood.*

10. Telephone interview with Robert Mawire, September 2003.

11. Meredith, *Another Country*, 191.

12. Saunders, *Never the Same Again.*

Chapter 2: Uniting Trade Unionists

1. Nkomo, *Story of My Life.*

2. Sachikonye, 'Trade Unions'.

3. Saunders, *Never the Same Again.*

4. My thanks go to Shari Eppel of the Amani Trust who explained this translation to me.

5. *Breaking the Silence: Building True Peace.* Published jointly by the Catholic Commission for Justice and Peace in Zimbabwe and the Legal Resources Foundation, Harare, February 1997; interview with Shari Eppel, July 2001.

6. *Breaking the Silence.*

7. Godwin, *Mukiwa,* 372.

8. Godwin, *Mukiwa.*

9. Sachikonye, 'Trade Unions'.

10. I am grateful to Alison Rudd for this story.

11. *The Chronicle,* 3 March 1989.

12. Interview with Wellington Chibebe, July 2002.

13. Interview with Wellington Chibebe, July 2002.

14. *Financial Gazette,* 27 June 1998.

15. *Financial Gazette,* 27 June 2000.

16. http://www.kubatana.net/html/archive/opin/ 050302dm.asp.

17. ZCTU Press Statement, 11 June 1992.

18. Tsvangirai quoted in Bond and Manyanya, *Zimbabwe's Plunge,* 85.

19. Bond and Manyanya, *Zimbabwe's Plunge,* 35.

20. Sachikonye, 'Trade Unions', 122.

21. Sachikonye, 'Trade Unions', 123.

22. *Sunday Mail*, 28 November 1993.

23. *Sunday Mail*, 6 February 1994.

24. *Sunday Mail*, 13 February 1994.

25. Bond and Manyanya, *Zimbabwe's Plunge*, 86.

26. Interview with Lovemore Madhuku, June 2004.

27. Saunders, *Never the Same Again*.

28. *Sunday Times*, 8 March 1999.

Chapter 3: Viva Democracy

1. Quoted by Tsvangirai in his speech at Rufaro Stadium, 19 June 2000.

2. Bond and Manyanya, *Zimbabwe's Plunge*.

3. Meredith, *Robert Mugabe*.

4. Website of the UK's Foreign and Commonwealth Office, http://www.fco.gov.uk/servlet/Front?pagename=OpenMarket/Xcelerate/ShowPage&c=Page&cid=1019745050212.

5. *Financial Mail*, 3 March 2000.

6. *Financial Mail*, 3 March 2000.

7. BBC News Online, 22 April 2000, http://www.bbc.news. co.uk.

8. BBC News Online, 22 April 2000.

9. *Time* Europe Online, 3 May 2000, http://www.time.com/time/europe/webonly/africa/2000/05/tsvangirai.html.

10. BBC News Online, 22 April 2000.

11. 'Summary of Political Violence in Zimbabwe since Referendum Result', 11 May 2000. Issued by the MDC Legal Committee.

12. BBC News, 26 April 2000.

13. BBC News Online, 28 April 2000.

14. BBC News Online, 28 April 2000.

15. BBC News Online, 8 May 2000.

16. 'Summary of Political Violence in Zimbabwe since Referendum Result', 11 May 2000. Statement of MDC Legal Committee.

17. BBC News, 12 May 2000.

18. Roger Pedersen, 'Report of the Norwegian Institute of Human Rights (Nordem)', November 2000.

19. *Business Day*, 22 May 2000.

20. ZW News, 23 May 2000, http://www.zwnews.com.

21. *Mail & Guardian*, May 2000.

22. *Independent* Online, as quoted by the MDC Mailing List, 1 June 2000.

23. BBC News Online, 31 May 2000.

24. BBC News, 7 June 2000.

25. BBC News, 7 June 2000.

26. My thanks to Kenyon Stirling, of Lawyers for Human Rights in Bulawayo, who related that many people had reported this phenomenon.

27. *The Star*, 12 June 2000.

28. *The Times*, 13 June 2000.

29. Statement issued by the National Democratic Institute for International Affairs (NDI), Washington, 20 June 2000.

30. *Independent*, 13 June 2000.

31. MDC Mailing List, 15 June 2000.

32. MDC Mailing List, 16 June 2000.

33. Freedom Speech, Rufaro Stadium, Harare, 19 June 2000.

34. Afrol.com, 24 June 2000, http://www.afrol.com/News/
zim024_elections_in_progress.htm.

35. BBC News Online, 6 July 2000.

36. Personal correspondence from Elizabeth Nelson, 2 July 2000.

37. *Guardian*, 8 November 2000.

38. *The Times*, 15 December 2000.

39. *The Times*, 15 December 2000.

40. *The Times*, 11 October 2000.

41. 'Politically Motivated Violence in Zimbabwe, 2000–2001'.
A report on the campaign of political repression conducted by
the Zimbabwean government under the guise of carrying out
land reform. Harare, Zimbabwe Human Rights NGO Forum,
2001.

42. BBC News Online, 7 May 2000.

43. Associated Press, 12 June 2000.

Chapter 4: The Presidential Election

1. Probe Market Research, a Gallup subsidiary. Quoted in
Johnson, 'Report on the election', 19 March 2002,
http://www.zimbabwesituation.com/apr7-2002.html.

2. Zimbabwe Human Rights NGO Report, October
2001–February 2002.

3. Norway Observer Mission, Preliminary Statement,
12 March 2002.

4. R.W. Johnson, 'Report on the election'.

5. Probe Market Research, a Gallup subsidiary. Quoted in Johnson, 'Report on the election'.

6. Johnson, 'Report on the election'.

7. Johnson, 'Report on the election'.

8. Johnson, 'Report on the election'.

9. *The Times*, 29 March 2002.

Chapter 5: The Aftermath

1. *The Guardian*, 19 March 2002.

2. *The Guardian*, 19 March 2002.

3. 'Final report on the Presidential Election in Zimbabwe 9–11 March 2002', Commonwealth Observer Group, http://www.kubatana.net/html/archive/elec/020331commwrep.asp?sector=ELEC&range_start=241.

4. *The Daily Telegraph*, 20 March 2002.

5. BBC News Online, 20 March 2002.

6. SABC News, 26 March 2002.

7. *Independent* Online, 23 March 2002, http://www.iol.co.za.

8. *Daily News*, 23 March 2002.

9. News24, 9 April 2002, http://www.news24.com.

10. *The Times*, 9 August 2002.

11. BBC News, 14 January 2003.

12. *Washington Post*, 15 January 2003.

13. *Daily News*, 19 March 2003.

14. 'Playing with Fire: Personal Accounts of Human Rights Abuses Experienced by Members of Parliament in Zimbabwe

and 28 Opposition Candidates.' Report commissioned by
The Zimbabwe Institute, Johannesburg, 2004.

15. *Sunday Times*, 22 June 2003.

16. Telephone interview with David Coltart, 2 September 2003.

17. Newsletter published by David Coltart, http://www.zvakwana.
org/html/prev/2003/nl/030903_038.shtml.

Chapter 6: Is this Treason?

1. On 28 February 2002, Tsvangirai launched legal action
against SBS Television in the New South Wales Supreme
Court. At the time of writing, SBS had agreed to an out-of-
court settlement, but for the case to be finalised in court, the
MDC has to pay a sum of A$120 000 – funds that the party
does not have.

2. *The Guardian*, 26 February 2002.

3. 'Ben-Menashe exposed', *Daily News*, http://www.zimbabwe
situation.com/feb24_2002.html.

4. *The Guardian*, 4 February 2003.

5. *Mail & Guardian* Online, 4 February 2003, cited on the
Zimbabwe Information Centre website, http://www.zic.com.
au/updates/2003/4february2003.htm.

6. *Mail & Guardian* Online, 4 February 2003, cited on the
Zimbabwe Information Centre website.

7. *Daily News*, 4 February 2003.

8. *Mail & Guardian*, 5 February 2003.

9. BBC News Online,
http://news.bbc.co.uk/1/hi/world/africa/2724645.stm.

10. Judgment document, *The State v. Morgan Tsvangirai*, High Court of Zimbabwe, Garwe JP, Harare, 3 February 2003 – 26 February 2004 and 15 October 2004.

11. *Mail & Guardian*, 5 February 2003.

12. Report of the trial on iafrica.com, 5 February 2003, http://www.iafrica.com.

13. *Jerusalem Post*, 1992.

14. Stephen Emerson in the *Wall Street Journal*, November 1992, http://www.jonathanpollard.org/1999/012299b.htm.

15. *Zimbabwe Independent*, 6 February 2003. Bizos was specifically referring to the fact that in 1997 and 1998 Ben-Menashe was paid US$7,8 million for maize procurement by the Zambian government. The maize was apparently never delivered (*The Daily News*, 22 April 2002).

16. ZW News, 13 February 2003.

17. Judgment document, *The State v. Morgan Tsvangirai*, High Court of Zimbabwe, Garwe JP, Harare, 3 February 2003 – 26 February 2004 and 15 October 2004: 11.

18. *Mail & Guardian*, 18 February 2003.

19. *Mail & Guardian*, 18 February 2003.

20. *Business Day*, 21 February 2003.

21. *Business Day*, 21 February 2003.

22. Voice of America Online, 21 February 2003.

23. *Daily News*, 20 May 2003.

24. *Business Day*, 26 June 2003.

25. SABC News, 26 June 2003.

26. *Sunday Times*, 10 August 2003.

27. *Mail & Guardian*, 11 February 2004.

28. ZW News, 12 February 2004.

29. News24, 25 February 2004.

30. News24, 25 February 2004.

31. *The Scotsman*, 26 February 2004.

Epilogue

1. Interview with George Bizos, March 2005.

2. Interview with George Bizos, March 2005.

3. All of the quotations attributed to Justice Garwe in this Epilogue are drawn from *The State v. Morgan Tsvangirai*, High Court of Zimbabwe, Ref. HH 169-2004 CRB224/02 (The judgment).

Postscript

1. *The Times*, 2 April 2005.

2. *Daily News* Online, Harare, 12 April 2005.

Select Bibliography

Bond, Patrick and Masimba Manyanya. *Zimbabwe's Plunge: Exhausted Nationalism, Neoliberalism and the Search for Social Justice*. Second edition. Pietermaritzburg and London: University of Natal Press and The Merlin Press, 2002.

Chikhuwa, Jacob W. *The Rise to Nationhood*. London: Minerva, 1998.

Godwin, Peter. *Mukiwa: A White Boy in Africa*. London: Macmillan, 1996.

Meredith, Martin. *The Past Is Another Country: Rhodesia 1890–1979*. London: André Deutsch, 1979.

Meredith, Martin. *Robert Mugabe: Power, Plunder and Tyranny in Zimbabwe*. Second edition. Johannesburg: Jonathan Ball, 2002.

Moorcraft, Paul L. *A Short Thousand Years*. Johannesburg: Galaxie, 1980.

Nelson, Harold D., ed. *Zimbabwe: A Country Study*. Second edition. Washington DC: American University, 1983.

Nkomo, Joshua. *The Story of My Life*. Second edition. Harare: Sapes Press, 2001.

Sachikonye, Lloyd. 'Trade Unions: Economic and Political Development in Zimbabwe since Independence in 1980'.

In Raftopoulos and Phimister, *Keep on Knocking: A History of the Labour Movement in Zimbabwe.* Harare: ZCTU, Friedrich Ebert Stiftung, Baobab Books, 1997.

Saunders, Richard. *Never the Same Again: Zimbabwe's Growth towards Democracy, 1980–2000.* Harare: Edwina Spicer Productions, 2001.

Smith, Ian. *The Great Betrayal: The Memoirs of Africa's Most Controversial Leader.* London: Blake, 1997.

Index